Deutsche Bank ▱

The publisher gratefully acknowledges Deutsche Bank for its support

THE MUMBAI NATURE GUIDE

THE MUMBAI NATURE GUIDE

SUNJOY MONGA

INDIA BOOK HOUSE PVT LTD

CONTENTS

INTRODUCTION 8

FOREST 17
Sanjay Gandhi National Park 18
Chinchoti & Tungareshwar 28
Kohoj 32
Jawahar 34
Elephanta Island 37
Tansa Wildlife Sanctuary 40
Matheran 42
Karnala Bird Sanctuary 46
Phansad Wildlife Sanctuary 48

SAHYADRI HILLS 51
Karjat 52
Khopoli-Pali Road 58

Lonavala & Khandala 60
Mahabaleshwar 62
Malshej Ghat 68
Bhimashankar 72

SCRUB & GRASS 75
Aarey Milk Colony 76
All India Radio Station 80
Talzan 82
Panvel 84
Bassein Fort & Naigon 86

COAST & WETLAND 89
Malad Creek 90
Manori Creek, Gorai & Uttan 94
Nirmal & Kelve 98

Sewri   101
Thane Creek   102
Uran   105
Mandwa, Alibaug
  & Murud-Janjira   110

URBAN SITES   115
Esselworld   116
IIT Campus
  & Powai Lake   118
Pirojshanagar (Godrej Estates)   120
Maharashtra Nature Park   122
Juhu Aerodrome &
  Bhavan's College Campus   124
Veermata Jijabai Bhonsle
  Udyan (Byculla Zoo)   125

Mahalaxmi Racecourse
  & Willingdon Sports Club   126
Malabar Hill   127
Sagar Upwan & Colaba Woods   128

APPENDIX   129
  Contacts   130
  Species Listing   130
  Mumbai's Green Heritage   136
  Some Rare Trees in Mumbai   136
  The Baobab   137

CONVERSIONS   137
CREDITS   138
ACKNOWLEDGEMENTS   138
INDEX   139

Introduction

On India's western sea-front lies the crowded
metropolis of Mumbai, well linked to
virtually every part of the country and the
world, with scores of scenic destinations in
its vicinity. The sites featured in this book fall
within a 150 km radius of the city. Although
Mahabaleshwar and Bhimashankar in the
Sahyadri lie outside this area, they are
nevertheless included on the strength of their
flora and fauna, and immense popularity.
Defined by the Konkan coast to the west and
the Sahyadri Hills of the Western Ghats to
the east, the northern limit of the area
selected is lined by the low hills of Jawahar,
while coastal Murud and Agardanda mark its
southern extent.

Lying on what is considered the outer
spur of the Western Ghats, the Mumbai
region is endowed with a rich biodiversity.
It enjoys a heavy monsoon and an exciting
mix of habitats that range from forests, grass,
scrub, hills and lakes, to sandy beaches,
mangrove creeks and mud-flats. Some sites
are polluted and threatened by tremendous
developmental pressures, yet nature displays
amazing resilience. These diverse habitats
host almost 1500 species of flowering plants,
nearly 360 of birds, at least 36 mammalian
and over 50 reptilian species, 160 varieties
of butterflies and over 200 kinds of fish.

An eagle majestically soars at the edge of the Sahyadri.

The Sahyadri Hills are a system of stratified basalt trap, dark igneous rocks, covered by laterite and clay. Characterized by steep escarpments, and often topped by flat plateaus, these weather-beaten cliffs and pinnacles lend a rugged charm to the landscape. The hills are often encrusted with dense forest, usually stunted in the windswept higher reaches. These lofty, basalt columns are not just popular with the rock-climbing and rappelling fraternity, but are also the favourite haunts of majestic Peregrine (Shaheen) Falcons, Alpine Swifts and kestrels. Numerous rivers originate in these ancient mountains, and flow through the plains of Konkan on their short westward journey to the Arabian Sea. Close to the coast, they transform into sluggish creeks inundated with sea water, with mangroves along the edges. The mangroves of the Mumbai region are among the larger surviving patches in the country. Nearly all the rivers are rain-fed, and once the monsoon arrives in early June, they gush down mountain slopes in short-lived grandeur. The damming of many of these waterways has created several reservoirs in the Konkan, Sahyadri and Deccan Plateau. These reservoirs meet the agricultural, industrial and domestic needs of the narrow, north Konkan belt, and also influence the aquatic life in their

Mixed deciduous forest (above) *dominates the Mumbai region, while moist evergreen trees* (facing page) *are seen in the sheltered valleys and upper reaches of the Sahyadri.*

immediate vicinity, drawing a multitude of waterside birds, including congregations of migratory waterfowl.

The region's long sea-front and wide coastal shelf support a wealth of marine life. Dolphins are occasionally sighted, while there is a solitary report of the Finless Black Porpoise. The Whale Shark is sometimes washed ashore and there are over 150 species of marine fish, nearly 200 of gastropods, 100 of bivalves, and more than 30 of crabs. Sadly, the marine zones have suffered immensely due to pollution and uncontrolled fish trade, and experts believe that up to one-third of the region's marine diversity could be irrevocably lost. This includes the critical habitat of mangroves, commonly perceived as wasteland, and sacrificed largely to reclamation schemes.

Locally known as *khari*, mangroves are tropical trees that grow in thickets, along with associate shrubs and other plants, by the side of creeks and mud-flats. On sheltered coastlines, they can form impregnable jungles, their tangled empire of aerial roots trapping organic matter that flows down from rivers, supporting a baffling array of life-forms. The Mumbai region contains an estimated 23 species of mangroves – the most abundant being White Mangrove (*Avicennia marina*). Mangroves can even be found growing within Mumbai city. Thane Creek has the largest mangrove cover (over 2200 ha) in the region. Mangroves also grow along Malad, Manori,

Bassein and Mahim Creeks, Sewri and Elephanta island. Small patches occur along Bandstand and Carter Road promenades in Bandra, and around Cuffe Parade and Navy Nagar in Colaba.

The flora of the Mumbai region is influenced to a great degree by its climate and diverse habitats, and to some extent by the human hand that has introduced many species. Several of these planted trees, shrubs, herbs and grasses have established themselves, and have, in fact, become quite abundant. Much of the forest is mixed-deciduous, interspersed and edged with plenty of bamboo. There is a sprinkling of semi-evergreen in the valleys and along stream-beds, and evergreen forests are found on hilltop sites such as Mahabaleshwar, Matheran, Bhimashankar and Malshej Ghat, which experience heavy rainfall. There is a wide range of herbs and shrubs, and many are annuals that erupt into view during monsoon, between June and October. Grass and reed-beds abound in the marshy tracts of Uran, which experiences some ingress of sea water, and is dotted with rain-filled depressions. The urban areas of Mumbai and Thane have a

surprisingly rich tree variety. Excluding the large forested tract of Sanjay Gandhi National Park, nearly 350 species of trees occur here, some of them scattered over Malabar Hill, the restricted area of Trombay across Sewri, and Elephanta island.

Despite this diversity, the original flora of the region is shrinking due to relentless development demands, and perhaps partly due to planting of exotic species. While various flowering and fruiting trees planted along roadsides and other areas have enhanced the bird and insect life,

purely ornamental flora does not support an adequate number of species. Areas such as the base of the Sahyadri Hills are being continually altered by a burgeoning number of private farms and orchards. In the scrub and grass around, numerous exotic species such as Common Lantana, Brazil Jute, Congress Grass and Castor Oil Plant have spread widely at the cost of some original flora.

Groves of coconut and Palmyra, miles of tall Casuarina, on which the occasional White-bellied Sea Eagle still nests, have been planted along the coastal tracts. Remnants of seaside flora are sporadically present in the less disturbed coastal stretches, from Gorai to Kelve in the north, and Alibaug to Murud in the south. Patches of flower cultivation add a splash of colour on the otherwise sandy brown coast.

While it is imperative that the endemic flora of our forests and mangrove creeks be preserved, judicious planning is required for introducing trees and shrubs in our urban areas, with more emphasis on endemic rather than ornamental flora.

Monsoon clouds build up over the coast (left). *A fruit bat feasts on custard apple in a city park* (top).

Every season brings change, profoundly influencing the flora and fauna of an area. The region of Mumbai is enchanting in all seasons, but it is probably the finest in winter, the period between mid-November and mid-February when there is an influx of wintering migrants, and flamingos arrive in full force in Sewri and Thane Creek. Although winter is extremely mild in the plains and on the coast, the hills are cool. As the monsoon verdure thins and turns a tawny gold, mammal sightings become more frequent, and pugs of Leopard, Sambar and other animals are seen at the edge of shrinking waterholes. The forests resound with the rutting calls of Spotted Deer (Chital) and Barking Deer. Red Silk Cotton and Flame of the Forest are in bloom, and become sites of considerable bird activity. This is also the ideal time to view mudskippers, crustaceans and other marine life along the coast.

The short transition month between winter and summer is marked by the birdsong of Magpie Robin and White-throated Kingfisher. Waders start to congregate, and woodpeckers and Grey Indian Hornbills are well into breeding. As the Indian Coral and Bonfire Tree burst into bloom, the fresh young leaves of Kusum trees add a crimson glow to the forest. Along creek edges, congregations of fiddler crabs emerge in large groups.

Summer, from mid-March to mid-June, is hot and humid in the plains, and not much more comfortable in the forested hills of the Sahyadri. Except for the evergreen species, many trees are devoid of leaves, making animal and bird sightings even easier. Waterholes, specially, exhibit tremendous activity. By the month of May, the last of the flamingos have departed and many woodland, scrub and ground birds have laid eggs or are tending their young. It is the courting season for several reptiles too, and the male

Forest Calotes is vivid in scarlet and black. Cicadas are highly vocal, and butterflies such as Spots Swordtail and Common Bluebottle mud-peddle around damp ground and puddles. The Indian Laburnum is in bloom and, with the pre-monsoon showers, Pink-striped Trumpet and Forest Spider Lilies magically erupt into view.

The landscape turns lush green in the monsoon months between mid-June and September, and there is a range of flowers, including begonias on rocky hillsides and near waterfalls. There is a glut of insects, and most birds have young in their nests. Cuckoos and warblers are highly vocal in this

The lanky Purple Heron (facing page) *can be occasionally sighted on marshes. The Sambar* (above) *keeps to the forested, hilly tracts in the Mumbai region.*

season, and amphibians loudly proclaim their readiness to mate. Mammal sightings are few, but in the soft, slushy mud, pugs are easy to spot. There have been several sightings of the female Leopard with cubs between July and September. The few resident waterfowl breed around freshwater marshes, lakes and ponds.

The post-monsoon season between late September and early November is a riot of colour. The vivid blooms of balsams, Graham's Groundsels, Sensitive Smithias, Oriental Sesames, Devil's Claw, Silver Spiked Cockscomb and many other annuals carpet the landscape. There is frenzied activity among the insects and as many as 40 species of butterflies can be sighted in a few hours. Many juvenile grass and scrub as well as forest birds are seen and, the winter migrants have already arrived in full force.

Here then is a region that, long cocooned by rugged mountains in the east and the eternal sea to the west, has been trapped in the vicious tentacles of development for the last twenty-five years. The population density in Mumbai is at par with the highest in the world, and vehicular traffic and pollution is overwhelming. Yet the city and the surrounding region have managed to retain a bit of nature within their fold. It is now up to its citizens to come to the region's aid and help preserve its natural splendour wherever possible, because this, as we now realize, is what makes both ecological and economic sense.

Many of the sites can be easily accessed by roads (left). *The Indian Laburnam in bloom* (top).

FOREST

Sanjay Gandhi National Park

North Mumbai; 27 km to Borivli main gate

SANJAY GANDHI NATIONAL PARK extends over 103 sq km, encircled by the congested suburbs of Mumbai and the adjoining district of Thane. The Bassein Creek divides its forests into two unequal parts, the smaller Nagla block lying to the north of the creek.

The park's hilly terrain is often regarded to be an outer spur of the Western Ghats. From almost sea level at Bassein Creek, the park's elevation rises to 486 m. Heavy monsoon rains and a variety of habitats – miles of mixed-deciduous forest with pockets of semi-evergreen, the expansive Vihar and Tulsi lakes, cactus-strewn rocky plateaus, scrub, marsh and creek – support a wealth of flora and fauna. Over 800 flowering plant species and nearly 150 varieties of butterflies are listed here. Of the 284 avifaunal species thus far recorded in the park, sometimes as many as 75 can be sighted within three hours on a winter morning. Over one-third of these bird species are seasonal visitors between October and April.

Small herds of Spotted Deer or Chital, the less sociable Sambar, little primate troops, and the usually solitary Common Mongoose may sometimes be encountered on the park's many walking trails. Barking Deer and Mouse Deer are less frequently seen. The Leopard, however, is omnipresent, and it has

The Leopard, an expert tree-climber, sometimes reveals itself on the park's many walking trails.

been occasionally spotted ambling along forest paths by day. The settlements on the park's periphery have brought it into increasing conflict with humans, and there have been over 75 casualties since 1986. The 50 reptilian species in the park include Mugger or Marsh Crocodile, more common in Tulsi Lake than Vihar; Bengal Monitor and the small Saw-scaled Viper, seen basking on the rocky plateau of Kanheri in winter; Indian Cobra and the crepuscular Russell's Viper.

The Owl Moth is often seen on rock-faces, and along damp mudbanks near streams.

SOUTH GATE TRAIL   *South gate to Vihar Lake, 2.5 km. Permission required* ▶▶
The first kilometre of this trail along the park's main, paved road, traverses scrub and light forest dominated by exotic deciduous trees such as Spotted Gliricidia and Copper Pod, introduced to the park over the last three decades. Taller, endemic species take over near the Pongam slope, roughly midway on the trail. The small rock-face before Pongam is the haunt of the giant Owl Moth, its wingspan measuring up to 15 cm, and there are chances of sighting the colourful Fungoid Frog in rainy weather.

The park resounds with the rutting cries of Barking Deer and Chital in winter. The timid Mouse Deer, which usually goes unnoticed due to its small size and protective colouration, was sighted here along with a fawn by some naturalists in May 2003. In the small defunct quarry, barely 200 m from the gate, pugs indicate the presence of Leopards and Small Indian Civets. Signs of the wallowing Sambar are occasionally visible here, as on the Vihar lakeside, while the dug up patches of earth indicate the omnivorous Wild Boar searching for tubers, roots, crops and insects.

Larger than Tulsi Lake to its north, Vihar's open, grassy banks are an ideal habitat for several open-land birds, including the Red-wattled Lapwing, and a few larks and pipits. The Malabar Pied Hornbill and the highly endangered Great Hornbill, birds of the neighbouring Western Ghats, were first sighted in the forest around Vihar Lake in February 2000. Other uncommon sightings include Eurasian Hobby, Black-

Closed to vehicular traffic, the tar road near Culvert 13 is overrun by monsoon herbage.

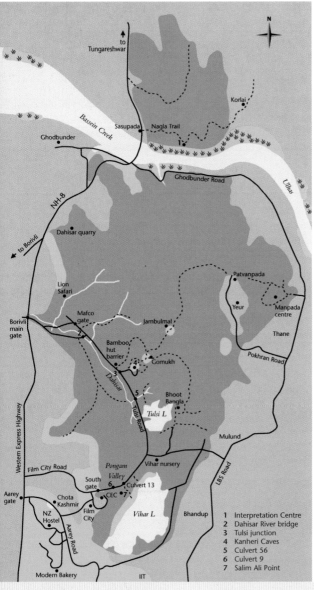

naped Oriole and Grey-headed Fish Eagle, as well as an isolated report of Amur Falcon from central Asia. A solitary Lesser Adjutant, a large, lanky stork found in eastern India, was also seen here in 2001. In winter, the lake attracts a variety of waterfowl, seen very close to the western margins on cold, wintry mornings. The resident Lesser Whistling Duck can be seen on the lake at dusk, whistling as it arrives to feed. The Night Heron and Brown Fish Owl also emerge amid a flurry of birds, and small herds of Chital, Wild Boar, and the odd Leopard and Sambar appear from the forest cover.

Side trails include an exploration of the hill north of the small quarry site near the gate, the stretch from Culvert 9 to Salim Ali Point, and the descent into Pongam Valley.

1 Interpretation Centre
2 Dahisar River bridge
3 Tulsi junction
4 Kanheri Caves
5 Culvert 56
6 Culvert 9
7 Salim Ali Point

FOREST   MANGROVE   MOUNTAIN   TRAIL   RAILWAY

GRASS & SCRUB   WATER   URBAN   ROAD   *The maps are not to scale*

Close to the south gate of the national park is Bombay Natural History Society's Conservation Education Centre (CEC), amid a 13-ha forested realm. The January-February blooms on the small cluster of Red Silk Cotton trees around its building attract several birds, including the odd Greater Racket-tailed Drongo. The CEC organizes nature programmes, and a visit can be combined with walks to Salim Ali Point and Vihar Lake.

ON TULSI ROAD

Tulsi junction to Tulsi Lake, 3 km. Permission required ▶▶

The Pink-striped Trumpet Lilies erupt in glorious blooms with the first monsoon showers of early June. In the park, the largest patch of these enormous flowers is found some 300 m from Tulsi junction. Along this forested trail, sightings of woodland birds are ample, especially in winter when nearly 50 species including several drongos, woodpeckers and flycatchers can be observed. Early morning is the best time to sight the Leopard padding down the tarred road that weaves through the forest. Though motorable, permission is seldom given for driving down this road.

Roughly midway on the trail, around the rocky, open land near Culvert 56, a huddle of flowering Red Silk Cotton trees is a magnet for birds between December and March. Near this

The showy, large flowers of Pink-striped Trumpet Lily bloom for a very short period in June (above). Post monsoon, the gregarious Common Marsh Buckwheat (centre) flowers along the Vihar Lake margins (top), a haven for birds after the rains.

In recent years, the Rufous Woodpecker has become the most widespread of the park's woodpeckers.

culvert, a fine birding trail ascends to the left towards the Buddhist caves of Kanheri, while another to the west leads to a secluded monsoonal waterfall and a grassy rock which commands a panoramic view of the Kanheri Ridge.

Fringed by thick forest, the dammed Tulsi Lake lacks the open environs of Vihar, and hosts fewer waterfowl. The fish-eating Osprey glide over the lake's surface in winter, and in summer, when the water level recedes, crocodiles may be seen basking on rocky outcrops. At the far end of the Tulsi dam is a narrow stone trench that leads into the Tulsi valley, a majestic sight from Kanheri Ridge. Covered for nearly half its 1.2 km length, it is popularly known as the Tunnel Trail. Around 1874, when the lake was created, this trench was constructed along the base of the slopes to optimize water collection from the catchment areas. A walk along the open stretch of the trail provides an excellent eye-level view of the forest floor. A searchlight is recommended for the covered area crowded with reptiles, spiders and insects, and there are a small number of bats as well. The Leopard and the Common Palm Civet are sometimes caught in the beam of the searchlight.

KANHERI TRAIL   *Tulsi junction to upper plateau, 2 km*
A considerable length of this narrow trail amid Kanheri Hills is along a rocky stream-bed that gushes and froths with rain water in the monsoon, creating small waterfalls alive with amphibian activity and providing a haunt for the blue-black Malabar Whistling Thrush. The tall deciduous forest around the

stream is rich in woodland bird species, an ideal spot to observe the arboreal and highly vocal Spangled Drongo, a sporadic seasonal visitor. This initial stretch of the trail gives way to a grass- and cactus-encrusted lower rocky plateau above Kanheri Caves.

Solitary stags or small herds of Sambar, the largest Indian deer, are occasionally sighted along Tulsi Road.

A climb that starts 500 m away leads to the upper plateau near Gomukh, its southern rocky overhang affording panoramic views of the park. This is a popular site for rappelling, and a good place to observe soaring raptors, especially the Peregrine (Shaheen) Falcon which has been seen feeding on parakeets and doves. A short diversion to the left of the Kanheri trail, roughly midway between the lower and upper plateaus, leads to a grass-covered rocky site excellent for watching nightjars, Blue Rock Thrush and Black-naped Hare.

TULSI VALLEY TRAIL

Kanheri Caves ticket counter to Vihar nursery, 7 km. Permission required ▶▶

The longest trail in the park begins at the Kanheri ticket counter, traversing densely forested hills that descend southwards from the top of Gomukh to the Tulsi Valley, and then leads on to the Vihar nursery. A charming stretch through fine deciduous forest, it is an ideal Sambar habitat, wild and rugged

in parts and with spectacular views of Tulsi Lake, particularly from the ruins of Bhoot Bangla, the residence of the engineer who supervised the Tulsi dam project in the 1870s. It is situated on a low hillock about 2.5 km from Gomukh, and from here a crocodile or two may be sighted, lazily drifting in the waters. Small herds of Chital are regularly seen, sometimes in association with langur monkeys on treetops, their warning cries alerting the deer to the presence of a leopard. Unlike the Sambar, which usually feed at night, the Chital is often seen feeding in daylight.

The walk south from Bhoot Bangla to the Tulsi waterworks at Thakurpada is along the more open eastern margins of the lake, frequented by a few waterbirds. This is where a Great Cormorant was first sighted in the park in July 2003. The last stretch from Thakurpada to the nursery, close to the Tulsi Road, is through scrub and light forest and an abundance of Hedge Caper, a shrub whose leaves are the food plant of numerous butterflies and moths. It is a likely site for Leopard, usually seen around dusk.

Spotted Deer are commonly seen in the park (right). *In summer and after monsoon, Common Blue Bottle butterflies can be seen mud-peddling at damp spots* (centre). *Bhoot Bangla in summer, situated in one of the park's finest deciduous forest patches* (top).

HIGHEST POINT TRAIL

Bamboo hut barrier to Jambulmal, 4.5 km. Permission required ▶▶

The trail to Jambulmal, the highest point (486 m) in the park, winds through dense deciduous forest. Roughly 2.5 km from the starting point, a path leads off left, partly along a rocky stream-bed. This route is made even more enchanting in March and April by the scarlet-yellow bloom clusters of evergreen Ashoka trees. The name 'Jambulmal' is believed to be derived from the presence of the evergreen *jambul* (Marathi for Jamun or Black Plum). Anjan is another evergreen tree seen at the mountain top.

A range of woodland birds is sighted on this trail, with a fair chance of observing the very melodious Brown-cheeked Fulvetta. Four of the park's five sightings of Malabar Trogon, a colourful arboreal native of the Western Ghats, have occurred on this trail. Six of the nine amphibian species in the park are reported here; they include the Ornate Narrow-mouthed, Fungoid and Short-headed Burrowing Frogs.

In the monsoon, Jambulmal is carpeted with lush herbage. The tall Karvi is the park's most abundant shrub whose purple flowers appear once every eight years. A few ground orchids bloom between late August and September, one of very few sites for these rather peculiar flowers. At the mountain top, as raptors soar and dip, a panoramic view of the forested Tulsi Valley and Tulsi and Vihar Lakes greets the eye. The shimmering Powai Lake and sprawling suburbs are seen in the distance.

Left to right: Harvester Ant nests are often seen on forest trails on the way to Jambulmal, the highest point in the park. Dainty ground orchids in bloom. The colourful flowers of the evergreen Ashoka tree in March and April.

SILONDA TRAIL *Near Mafco gate to seasonal waterfall, c. 3.5 km. Permission required* ▶▶

The Silonda trail starts about 200 m from the Mafco gate to cross dense deciduous forest, with patches of evergreen near the stream-beds, and leads in the direction of Kanheri Ridge. A heavy downpour in the monsoon transforms the dry stream-beds into surging rapids.

The Yam Fly is a brightly coloured butterfly whose larvae feed on the Yam plant.

The high tally of 70 bird species recorded on the trail includes Emerald Dove, Forest Wagtail, Spangled Drongo, Heart-spotted Woodpecker, and a solitary sighting of the rare Malabar Trogon. The moss-encrusted rocks near the waterfall sprout a few tiny pale pink Common Begonia flowers. In the rains, the forest floor is crammed with dainty red mushrooms, and the fluty call of the Malabar Whistling Thrush resounds through the air. This is an excellent monsoon trail for observing insects.

DAHISAR QUARRY *Permission required*

Nature is slowly creeping back into the heavily eroded terrain of the Dahisar quarry, a 20-ha site restored to the forest department following a 1997 court order. Tree-plantation programmes along the barren slopes are yielding results. The several pools of water, both natural and man-made, draw the occasional civet and leopard. This is probably the foremost Mumbai site for Eurasian Eagle Owl and at least two breeding pairs have been seen here. Greater effort and intensive patrolling can convert this long-degraded terrain into a superb rocky habitat.

It is also possible to make a two-hour trek from this quarry site to the Lion Safari area in the tourism zone. Passing through bamboo, scrub and light forest, the walk is quite enjoyable during the rains.

Streams along the Silonda trail gush forth in short-lived glory during the monsoon, nurturing a wealth of life.

MANPADA CENTRE

Between August and October, waves of vivid yellow Sensitive Smithias and purple balsams carpet the slopes of the Manpada Centre. Located in the northeast region of the park, the centre is just off Ghodbunder Road, with Yeur Hills to the south. Its modest, but well-visited photo display highlights the park's rich biodiversity.

Laid to waste by quarrying activity, Manpada was salvaged in the 1970s and '80s with plantations of many tree varieties, several of them exotic, such as Australian Acacia, Su-babul, Copper Pod and Flamboyant (Gulmohur). Endemic species, such as Sissoo (Indian Rosewood) and Variegated Bauhinia, have lately been planted. Barking Deer and the occasional Leopard are among the few mammals that can sometimes be seen in the area.

MALAD PATROLLING TRAIL

Dahisar River bridge junction to BMC Reservoir, c. 4 km ▶▶

A well-laid trail that begins a few metres from the junction skirts the park's western periphery, passing through teak plantation and low secondary forest where bulbuls, warblers, flycatchers and babblers can be encountered, and occasionally birds of dense forest such as Greater Racket-tailed Drongo and Grey Junglefowl. Part of this trail lies close to human settlements and the Leopard is never very far away. It is also excellent for observing insects and spiders, and as many as seven varieties of praying mantis have been sighted.

NAGLA BLOCK & TRAIL   *North of Mumbai; 36 km to Sasupada hamlet* ▶▶

The 16 sq km Nagla block lies in the Thane district, north of the indolent Bassein Creek. Short, degraded mangroves at the creek's mouth, near Uttan-Bhayandar, give way to healthier growth fringed by tall forest as the creek winds inwards, traversing nearly 2 km of the park. The mangrove belt supports marine creatures such as mudskippers, crabs and fish, and attracts aquatic birds, including a few Clamorous Reed Warblers. A narrow, partly wooded stretch almost connects Nagla to the heavier forested tracts of Chinchoti and Tungareshwar in the north.

The popular Nagla trail begins at Sasupada hamlet on the Mumbai-Ahmadabad highway (NH-8) to end at Korlai village about 5 km away.

Numerous Sensitive Smithia flowers carpet the ground in the latter half of the monsoon (above). *The Eurasian Eagle Owl in the Dahisar quarry area* (top).

It first passes leafy forest and some of the park's tallest specimens of the deciduous Haldu. Pugs of civets, Leopard, Sambar and Wild Boar are sometimes encountered around waterholes, and the non-venomous Checkered Keelback Snake may be sighted. Nagla has fewer mammals than the southern segment of the park, but in May 2003 fresh tiger pugs were seen on its northern fringe. It is believed that the tiger entered via the Tungareshwar forest.

The scenic banks of the creek around the Interpretation Centre form a pleasant observation spot for waterside birds. The White-bellied Sea Eagle and the Osprey can be sighted in winter, these majestic aerial hunters closing in on their prey (fish or water snakes), seemingly oblivious to the din of hurtling highway traffic. Fewer woodland birds are seen here than in the southern section of the park.

The terrain turns somewhat rocky as the trail continues northeast towards Korlai and Nagla Bunder villages. On the left is bamboo, scrub and dense herbage with occasional clumps of tall trees. There is typical deciduous forest along the gradual incline towards Korlai Hill (260 m), the highest point in Nagla. To the right, mangroves fringe dense scrub as the trail skirts Bassein Creek. Then, as the trail curves to the northeast, the jungle suddenly opens out, providing a view of the creek's wide curve and its broad swathe of mangroves.

The Black-hooded Oriole is a regular sight in the forest (right). The scenic Bassien Creek along the trail (top).

CHINCHOTI & TUNGARESHWAR
North of Mumbai; 48 km to Chinchoti junction; 52 km to Tungareshwar junction

CHINCHOTI IS CLOTHED IN fairly healthy mixed-deciduous vegetation, almost a continuation of the Sanjay Gandhi National Park forest. It offers a rewarding two-hour walk from Chinchoti junction on NH-8 to a waterfall about 4 km away that springs to life only in rainy weather, when it hosts hordes of weekend visitors.

The predominantly open scrubland with scattered habitations along the first half of the trail support a sprinkling of open-land birds. Signs of mammals such as Jackal, Common Mongoose and Black-naped Hare may be observed. The Striped Hyena was last sighted here in 1995 and has since probably been hunted out of the area. The Leopard is seen occasionally.

In the summer of 2003, Tungareshwar, north of Chinchoti, shot into the limelight with the report of a tiger sighting. Its thick forests, burdened by an uncontrolled influx of visitors to its temple site, host at least 500 plant species and nearly 150 varieties of birds. With an area of about 85 sq km, Tungareshwar was declared a wildlife sanctuary in November 2003.

The approach to Tungareshwar, east of NH-8, is through a short, dreary stretch of habitation. Dry and dusty in summer, the lower reaches of Tungareshwar turn lush green with the first monsoon showers. A blanket of

A panoramic view of the north Konkan region from Tungareshwar's upper trail.

splendid evergreen forest covers the higher reaches. At 670 m, the Tungareshwar mountain is the highest point in north Konkan.

The site was recommended for a sanatorium as early as 1865, but apart from the scattered ruins of 19th-century British homes and a hotel, Tungareshwar retains much of its pristine charm, despite the crowds at the temple sites. *See map on page 36.*

LOWER TRAIL   *Tungareshwar junction to Mahadeo Temple, c. 3 km* ▶▶

A dusty, unpaved path gradually ascends Tungareshwar towards the Mahadeo Temple situated at a height of about 160 m. Part of the route is along a rocky stream-bed, bone-dry in summer, but a raging torrent during the monsoon. Although vehicles ply on this trail, treks are recommended. Treepies, drongos, barbets, orioles and leafbirds are typical of this mixed-deciduous forest, and the wary Grey Junglefowl is also present. Leopard, Rusty Spotted Cat and Common Palm Civet – one of the few civets that feed on wild fruit – are among the mammals observed or reported here. Narrow tracks branch off the main trail and lead through slender strips of semi-evergreen forest along the numerous steep ravines.

UPPER TRAIL   *Mahadeo Temple to Tungareshwar's summit, c. 7 km* ▶▶

The road above the temple is unpaved but motorable. However, a trek is recommended through the finest of Tungareshwar's forests to observe the dramatic change in vegetation, as deciduous fades into semi-evergreen and then evergreen forest, dark and deep, reminiscent of Matheran. The enormous rocks of the western face of the main ridge are visible from NH-8.

Most waterfalls here are highly seasonal, such as this one at Chinchoti (right). *The Mahadeo Temple* (top).

The views along the trail are spectacular. To the west, the plains arc from south of Bassein Creek to well north of Tansa River, with the glittering Arabian Sea beyond. About 5 km along the trail, at a height of 350 m, the Pelhar Lake shimmers into view through the forest deep below.

The varied avifauna includes Brown-cheeked Fulvetta, Shama, White-throated Thrush, Scarlet Minivet, hornbills, barbets and an unusually large population of Crested Serpent Eagle, an impressive predator distinguished by its shrill, penetrating screams. Pugs and scat on the loose red soil of the trail indicate the presence of Sambar, Barking Deer, Common Langur, Common Palm Civet, Common Mongoose and Leopard.

Cool breezes fan the small rocky plateau on top, its highest point marked by a rusty metal tower. Once a cactus- and rock-strewn landscape mined for bauxite, many evergreen varieties of the Sahyadri occur along Tungareshwar's upper reaches. It is not unusual to find Ground Lily and Hill Turmeric flowering in late summer, well before the first monsoon showers lash the region. A sizeable population of Atlas Moth is reported on Tungareshwar, the wingspan of these insects reaching up to 28 cm.

Dense evergreen forest along Tungareshwar's upper trail.

The ridge near Sadanand Ashram affords a panoramic view of Mahuli and Matheran ranges to the east, while Tansa River meanders across the cultivated plains below. To the north lies the Takmak mountain. The 5 km trail north of the *ashram* descends through dense forest to Vajreshwari Road that later joins the NH-8.

PELHAR LAKE
The small, dammed Pelhar Lake at the foot of Tungareshwar's main western ridge is just a few minutes' drive from Tungareshwar junction on NH-8. Human habitation and dense scrub characterize its landscape, with scrub and secondary growth encrusting the lake's periphery. There are very few waterside birds. A narrow ascending trail on the main ridge joins the upper trail leading to Sadanand Ashram, and heavy scrub gives way to tall mature forest.

TAKMAK MOUNTAIN & BHANDRE LAKE   *Nearby*
The large fort-topped Takmak mountain is roughly 15 km north of Tungareshwar. The thick forest at its base contrasts with the light cover in its rocky upper reaches. Further north is Bhandre Lake, from where the twin pinnacles on Takmak's eastern ridge are visible, but a trek to Takmak takes over three hours. In the monsoon, scrub and light forest around the reservoir is an excellent habitat for quails and cuckoos, both very vocal in this season.
Occasionally, Common Kestrel and Peregrine Falcon are sighted here.

Top to bottom: *The Crested Serpent Eagle at Tungareshwar indicates a healthy habitat. Tungareshwar hosts one of the largest populations of the Atlas Moth in the Mumbai region. A pair of predatory Robber Fly mating. Among the many wild flowers is the Forest Barleria, usually seen along trails.*

KOHOJ

North of Mumbai; 100 km to Nane village

AT THE VAITARNA RIVER BRIDGE on NH-8, the 570 m-high Kohoj looms to the east, beyond the languidly meandering river. A short distance away, a diversion to the right leads to the Silent Hill Resort, and a stroll through light forest and scrub along its eastern fringes ends at the confluence of the Vaitarna and its tributary, the Deheraja.

Returning to the bridge and soon passing Mastan junction, a road to the right – heading towards the hilly and predominantly tribal areas of Wada, Jawahar and Suriamal – leads to a bridge on the Deheraja River, a promising halt for viewing bitterns and rails, especially in the monsoon breeding season. The rains also bring swarms of blue-and-yellow striped Painted Grasshopper, seen feasting on the common Giant Milkweed shrub whose leaves secrete milky latex when plucked. The profusion of other insects at this time attracts lizards and praying mantis.

Just past the Deheraja River, light scrub yields to heavier forest and the towering form of Kohoj. At Hamrapur junction, a scenic back road to Kanchad leads off to the right, while immediately ahead lies the village of Vaghote, the base for a trek to Kohoj. Kohoj is topped by one of the several hill-forts of north Konkan. Occupied by the Portuguese in the early 16th

The verdant landscape of Kohoj is most beautiful during monsoon.

century, the fort passed from the Marathas to the British in the 18th century, and later fell to ruin. Reminiscent of the Sahyadri Hills, there is a belt of immense black igneous rock around Kohoj's extensive base. The broad lower slopes support reasonably healthy pockets of forest despite some lopping for firewood. *See map on page 36.*

AROUND KOHOJ

Hamrapur junction to Kanchad, 18 km ▶▶

This 18 km drive skirts the south face of Kohoj, passing through sparsely inhabited countryside. In the rainy season and till late October, emerald-green paddy fields and lush verdure carpet the landscape. The monsoon brings with it a plethora of insects, and on the halts along the way, gaudily-coloured beetles, bugs and grasshoppers, perhaps even a Bengal Monitor, Common Mongoose and some varieties of snake can be observed. In winter, birds of scrub and grass such as harriers, Short-toed Eagle, Common Kestrel, Black-headed Bunting, Stonechat and numerous larks can be sighted, besides the perennial bulbuls, warblers and bee-eaters. Mammals reported here include Jackal, Wild Boar, Black-naped Hare and the occasional Striped Hyena.

A motionless Cinnamon Bittern hides in monsoon vegetation (above). Gaudily-coloured Painted Grasshoppers are common between August and November (top).

KOHOJ FORT TREK   *Nane village to Kohoj Fort, c. 4 km* ▶▶

A trek to the fort from Nane village, on the 18 km Hamrapur junction-Kanchad route, takes the narrow track which traverses mixed-deciduous forest near the base and lower slopes. As compared to the trek from Vaghote village, the climb is rather steep. A sprinkling of woodland birds includes the sporadic Grey Junglefowl, last reported here in 2001.

SAJANPADA & DEVKOP LAKE   *Nearby*

Sajanpada, a fine stretch of low, forested hills, lies on the Manor-Palghar Road west of NH-8, just past Mastan junction. It resounds with calls of woodland birds, including the White-bellied Drongo, Black-hooded Oriole and Black-rumped Flameback. Small troops of Common Langur can be seen sometimes. Towards the western margins of this forest lies the tranquil Devkop Lake, situated on a small tributary of the Surya River and surrounded by wooded hills and secondary growth. In winter, migratory waterfowl such as Northern Pintail, Garganey and Common Teal, and scrubland birds are sighted.

JAWAHAR
North of Mumbai; 130 km to Jawahar town

THE PREDOMINANTLY HILLY TERRAIN OF JAWAHAR, east of NH-8, is the home of the Warlis, famous for their traditional painting style. A considerable part of this area is under cultivation, and the remaining forest tracts face agricultural encroachments and lopping for firewood, resulting in low mammal density. Jawahar lacks an adequate tourist infrastructure, but its attractions lie in the scenic, undulating countryside, particularly in the monsoon when waterfalls erupt and bone-dry stream-beds become raging torrents. The dull summer landscape is transformed by the green of paddy fields, and an empire of birds and insects feed off the abundant flowering plants.

EN ROUTE TO JAWAHAR & WADA
Pali junction to Jawahar, 24 km; Pali junction to Wada, 110 km
At Pali junction, the bifurcation on the road from Mastan junction to Wada traverses a distinctly rural setting towards Jawahar. The first halt is the sprawling Sajan Nature Club, a kilometre off the main road, which organizes bird-watching tours, visits to tribal settlements and treks to nearby sites such as Palusa Waterfall and Tiger Caves. The Moho-Khurd Dam, 2 km from the resort, draws a few waterfowl in winter.

The Gargai River sometimes retains pools of water during summer, drawing birds and animals.

The vegetation after Vikramgadh, a ten-minute drive from Sajan, is a mix of scrub and paddy cultivation. Ain and Mahua trees are common, and the dense Christ's Thorn is a widespread evergreen shrub, its tangy fruit relished by humans and birds alike. It is also a favourite of the Olive Green Hawkmoth. The tribals of this region distil a heady spirit from the cream-coloured, scented Mahua flowers that bloom between February and May.

The rock-strewn, uninhabited plateau, reached after a short ascent, a few kilometres from Vikramgadh, can be a brief birding halt. The stunted Ain trees and the profuse grass and scrub provide an ideal habitat for White-eyed Buzzard, Black-eared Kite, nightjars and chats, and the Black-naped Hare is quite common. With the onset of the monsoon, signs of cuckoos, babblers, quails, francolins and warblers become more frequent.

Jawahar is another 5 km away. From here, one can either head west towards Mumbai via tall deciduous forests and Surya Reservoir to Kasa, or travel east towards the heavily wooded tract between Suriamal and Wada, a northern spillover of the adjoining Tansa Wildlife Sanctuary. This picturesque, albeit circuitous, 110 km drive from Pali junction to

Top to bottom: The vividly coloured flowers of Glory Lily dot the landscape during August and September, and the flashy Indian Roller is seen in winter. The Spots Swordtail is one of the few spectacular butterflies active in summer. The start of the monsoon is sometimes marked by the appearance of red velvet mites.

In peak summer, the crimson-and-black Forest Calotes male shows off his colours to attract a mate (above). The Jawahar-Wada countryside (top).

Wada offers many opportunities for bird watching, and there is the odd chance of sighting mammals on the Suriamal–Wada stretch.

EN ROUTE TO SURIAMAL
Wada junction to Suriamal, 32 km

North of Wada, 9 km beyond Pali junction, open country is soon overtaken by deciduous forest, in the rains dark and overgrown with a riot of creepers and foliage, interspersed with paddy fields, and filled with birdsong. At Parli, midway to Suriamal, the road enters a substantial forest on the northern fringe of Tansa Wildlife Sanctuary. The Gargai River winds to the right, often hidden from view by thick foliage. During the gradual ascent to Suriamal, darting flycatchers and colourful minivets can be seen, as Red Spurfowl dash about and the skulking Scimitar Babbler is revealed by its melodious cries. Not far away, a Barking Deer calls. About 12 km from Parli, a short path on the right leads to the confluence of the Gargai with a small rivulet. The river-bed is almost bone-dry in summer but, during the monsoon spate, cries of Painted Francolin, cuckoos and other birds rent the air. The final 5 km to Suriamal is most rewarding on foot. Numerous raptors and fast-flying White-rumped Swift and Alpine Swift have been spotted here. The thick forest hosts few mammals, and those reported include primates, deer, Leopard, Rusty Spotted Cat and Small Indian Civet.

1 Silent Hill Resort
2 Hamrapur junction
3 Vaghote
4 Vaitarna River bridge
5 Vighaleshwar Lake
6 Nalla Sopara junction
7 Pelhar Lake
8 Tungareshwar junction

ELEPHANTA ISLAND
NE of Gateway of India; 10 km to main jetty from the Gateway

THE ISLAND OF ELEPHANTA, known to its inhabitants as Gharapuri, is a popular tourist attraction, famous for its ancient rock-cut cave temple dedicated to Lord Shiva. Two low hills, separated by a narrow valley, dominate this island of basalt trap, the larger eastern hill rising nearly 200 m above sea level. The slopes retain a bit of original forest, and Teak, Haldu, Bonfire Tree, Kino, Red Silk Cotton, Karaya, Flame of the Forest as well as other deciduous varieties are characteristic of the flora that once covered the Mumbai area. Among the approximately 300 plant species recorded here, nearly one-third constitutes introduced varieties such as Eucalyptus, Flamboyant (Gulmohur), Jacaranda, Mango and Tamarind. Shrubs and herbs grow copiously in the monsoon, and Shore Purselane and Sea Holly partly encrust the 6 km coastline, a mix of sand, mud-flats and rocky areas with sparse mangrove cover. However, the constant influx of visitors have taken their toll. Elephanta's coastline also faces continuous depredation as the island lies within the Mumbai harbour with industries nearby.

The best time to explore the island is on quiet weekdays, when the stream of visitors thins out. The hillsides play host to woodland birds and, between October and April, wintering waders such as Eurasian Oystercatcher and the

The hour-long boat journey to Elephanta island is a delightful escape from the city.

lanky Western Reef Egret, as well as Pallas's Gull and Caspian Tern may be seen. Numerous eagles, buzzards and hawks are quite easily sighted at Elephanta. At low tide, the exposed mud-flats, even along the main jetty, teem with marine life, including hermit crabs, fiddler crabs, mudskippers and other crustaceans and molluscs, attracting herons, kingfishers and a fair number of waders that also frequent the island's rocky southern coast. Small flocks of the migratory Greater and Lesser Flamingo have been sighted twice.

The island is plagued by its overwhelming primate population. It is feared that the large numbers of Bonnet Macaques may adversely affect the breeding of resident avifauna. Other mammals include Flying Fox, the largest of the Indian bats, which flies in from the mainland to feed on Elephanta's fruit-bearing trees, and the smaller and less common Bearded Sheath-tailed Bat.

ISLAND TRAIL   *Starts and ends at main jetty, c. 6 km*
The island is circumscribed by a track that serves as an excellent nature trail, starting a short way from the main jetty. It skirts Shet Bandar village, forested Canon Hill and the village of Bandargaon, before traversing the scrub and light forest of eastern Diyachi Dongar hill. The coast along the trail changes from rocky to sandy, and at times is edged by mangrove thickets.

Sightings of Oystercatcher, Curlew, Whimbrel and a host of smaller waders, gulls and terns are possible between October and April, when raptors such as the White-bellied Sea Eagle are also seen.

The island of Elephanta hosts a varied biodiversity. Migrant waders (left) assemble on the rocky and sandy shores, while fiddler crabs (top) are seen on mud-flats and ooze. Around the caves and over much of the island, armies of primates, dominated by Bonnet Macaques (above left), are the most visible of the mammals here.

BANDARGAON TRAIL

Main jetty to main cave entrance, c. 3.5 km

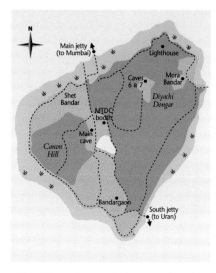

The island trail can be cut short before Bandargaon village by taking the well-trodden path through the narrow valley that separates the two hills. After cutting through light forest after Bandargaon, the trail edges around a small pond that attracts some herons, cormorants, kingfishers and bee-eaters in winter and early summer. The trail leads towards the entrance to the main cave. Several woodland birds are sighted on this walk – the resident Scarlet Minivet, Black-rumped Flameback and the uncommon White-bellied Drongo. The sprightly Paradise Flycatcher and the occasional blue-green Verditer Flycatcher are fascinating to watch as they launch short aerial sallies, in characteristic flycatcher-manner. A short 2 km trail near the main jetty leads to Caves 6 and 7 on the eastern hill, where the forest is relatively undisturbed.

The boat ride to Elephanta offers some close encounters with migrant gulls.

TANSA WILDLIFE SANCTUARY
NE of Mumbai; 100 km to Tansa rest-house

THE 320 SQ KM TANSA WILDLIFE SANCTUARY in Thane district is the largest protected area in the Mumbai region, its forests forming the catchment area for Tansa and Vaitarna reservoirs, which supply a third of Mumbai's water. Some roads lead off the Mumbai-Nashik highway (NH-3) into the sanctuary, a prime habitat on Shahpur Plateau, on an outer spur of the Sahyadri Hills. One of the finest routes is from Vashind, south of the reserve and 42 km from Thane. The northern parts of the sanctuary are best explored from Suriamal.

A forty-minute drive from Thane, via a creek, scrubland and cultivated fields, leads to the Mahuli Hills. Much of the sanctuary lies north of this isolated range, and extends for roughly 25 km to Suriamal. Over four hours of climbing takes the dedicated trekker to the ruins of a fort conquered by Shivaji, the Maratha leader, in the 17th century. Bird's-eye views of sprawling hills and the tranquil expanse of Tansa Lake are added reward.

Primarily a moist mixed-deciduous forest, the sanctuary has a diverse landscape of hills, ravines, lakes as well as the Tansa, Vaitarna and Gargai Rivers. Tigers roamed free in the area until the late 19th century, but were wiped out by indiscriminate hunting and the burgeoning demand for agricultural land. The Gaur, Dhole and Wolf have suffered the same fate.

The imposing, jagged hills of Mahuli loom over deciduous forests close to NH-3.

VASHIND TO TANSA REST-HOUSE *25 km*
The road branching left off NH-3 at Vashind passes
the small tribal settlements of Pipli, Vandre and
Aghai before reaching the Tansa rest-house. Scrub
and paddy cultivation appear intermittently along
a route shaded by dense deciduous forest that
typically comprises Teak, Myrobalan, Karaya, Flame
of the Forest, Haldu, Mahua, Karanj, Kusum and
Black Siris. In early summer, numerous flowering
trees add more than a dash of colour, and dense
clusters of pale green Paper Flower Climber are
seen sporadically in the canopy.

Even beyond the sanctuary's gate, about 12 km
from Vashind, the road is never entirely free of
traffic, but the trails on either side are quieter, their
silence broken only by bird calls. A path along a
rocky stream-bed to the right leads to the looming
Mahuli Hills, and explorations can be made on
foot. Huge pipelines that were part of
Mumbai's water distribution system
occur up to Aghai, nearly 10 km
from the gate. In the rains, this
forested stretch resounds with the
calls of cuckoos and warblers, and
small purple flowers of Common
Balsam sprout along the roadside.
Winter brings flocks of migrant
duck to the lakes, including Pintail,
Common Teal and Garganey. Walks
around the rest-house, 4 km from
Aghai, are ideal for observing birds.
A short trail leads to Tansa Lake
where, around dusk, Leopard, Small
Indian Civet and Indian Porcupine
have been seen. Birds of open scrub,
such as quails and francolins, are
more numerous along the 12 km
stretch from the rest-house to
Atgaon, on the NH-3, where Striped
Hyena has been recently reported.

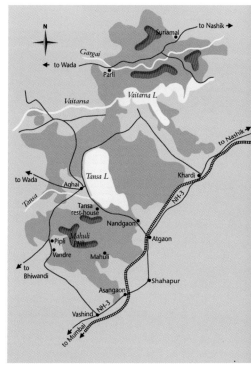

Greater Racket-tailed Drongo.

MATHERAN
East of Mumbai; 95 km to Dasturi car park

IN 1850, THE COLLECTOR OF THANE DISTRICT, Hugh Poyntz Malet, made a steep ascent via One Tree Hill from Chauk in the plains to the hilltop of Matheran, where he built a bungalow called 'The Byke'. Five years later, Matheran earned itself another zealous admirer – Lord Elphinstone, governor of Bombay. Soon, a roughly constructed road provided easy access to the elite of Bombay city.

In 1907, the quaint toy train from Neral made its first steep haul to the top, turning Matheran into an increasingly popular summer retreat. Yet, its air continues to be pure and its trails free of vehicular traffic. The credit goes largely to the Bombay Environment Action Group for bringing 215 sq km of Raigad district, including Matheran and adjoining Prabalgadh, under the Eco-sensitive Zone, thus prohibiting vehicles, plastic bags and all industrial activity in the area.

Motorable roads have not been made to Prabalgadh either, but an unmarked trek from the base of the hill explores its dense jungle-clad gullies and plateau. It is a short, steep drive from Neral to Matheran. The road terminates at the Dasturi car park and the only way to the top is on foot or horseback, or by hand-pulled cart. The plateau extends over 7.4 sq km and

Wild flowers on one of Matheran's enchanting points, with Prabalgadh in the background.

reaches an elevation of 803 m at Panorama Point. The vegetation transforms dramatically from near-barren plains and open deciduous forests to the dense semi-evergreen and evergreen jungles of the upper reaches, dominated by Anjan, Jamun, Hill Jambul, Indian Medlar and Kokam. Situated on a geographically separate hill range, Matheran nevertheless shares much of the character of the Sahyadri ecosystem. There is a profusion of herbs and shrubs, even more so during the monsoon.

A maze of bridle paths and trails, their soil a distinct red, twist and wind through Matheran. Nearly all the trails lead to famous lookout points at the edge of the cliffs, ideal for observing Common Kestrel, Peregrine Falcon and Alpine Swift in majestic flight. Undoubtedly, the best way to explore Matheran is on foot. The more secluded paths are unmarked, and others veer dangerously close to the edge, but clear-day views of the surrounding hills can be breathtaking. The Chanderi, Malanggad and Peb hills of the

Top to bottom: *From glistening, procreating beetles on the forest floor to perky, melodious bulbuls on flowering trees, from the enchanting toy train winding over 20 km to Matheran, to the serene Charlotte Lake in the forest, there are many interesting sights on this little mountain top.*

Matheran Range loom to the north, and Prabalgadh, Irshal, Manikgadh and Karnala are to the southwest. Panvel lies to the west, and the arc of the Sahyadri is to the east.

Matheran is the haunt of forest birds, and there is a wealth of drongos, bulbuls, babblers, flycatchers and thrushes. As the first rays of the sun brighten the eastern sky, the forest stirs to life with the loud calls of hidden junglefowl and the melodious notes of Shama. From Mumbai, Matheran is the closest natural site to resound with the rattling cries of the colourful Indian Giant Squirrel. It is a small population, perhaps even totally isolated, and these wary creatures are easier heard than seen. The highly elusive Small Indian Civet and Rusty-spotted Cat have been seen. In recent times, the Striped Hyena has been sighted along the foothills.

Matheran is enchanting in every season. Monsoon rains lash down furiously and the average of nearly 300 cm sees Charlotte Lake, the town's main water source, brim over. A thick mist can envelop the forest for days on end as birds, frogs and insects gear up for procreation. Post-monsoon, the air is crisp and cool, and the forest a sparkling green. However, the best period to visit is between November and March when there is an influx of wintering birds from the Himalaya and peninsular India. Cicadas rule the summer months, and the deafening chorus of the males is designed to attract mates, drowning all other jungle sounds.

Silvery streaks of cascading waters rush down mountain slopes during the torrential monsoon.

Distances from the station

WESTERN MATHERAN

Shivaji's Ladder	5 km
Belvedere Point	4 km
Charlotte Lake	2 km
Lord Point	2.5 km
Louisa Point	2.5 km
Coronation Point	2 km
Porcupine Point	2.5 km
Maldung Point	2 km
Monkey Point	2.5 km
Hart Point	3 km
Panorama Point	5 km

EASTERN MATHERAN

Garbut Point	4 km
Madhavji Point	1 km
Khandala Point	1.2 km
Alexander Point	2.5 km
Rambag Point	3.5 km
Little Chauk Point	4.5 km

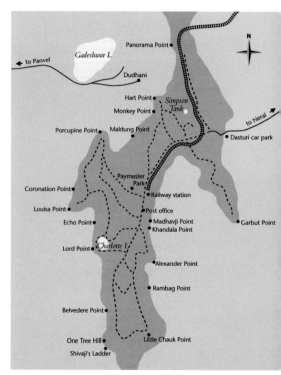

KARNALA BIRD SANCTUARY
SE of Mumbai; 50 km to forest office

THE BUSY MUMBAI-GOA HIGHWAY (NH-17) carves through the 12.11 sq km Karnala Bird Sanctuary, just 12 km south of Panvel. Dominated by a pinnacle 469 m high, several trails criss-cross the sanctuary, which hosts about 150 species of avifauna. The finest trails lie in the eastern, more hilly section, although the Boremal trail in the west is also an enjoyable walk. Against the din of traffic, the melodious Shama and the high-pitched calls of Greater Racket-tailed Drongo and several woodpeckers jostle for attention.

At the height of summer, breeding time for Crested Tree-swift, Pompadour Pigeon, Brown-headed Barbet and a host of other woodland birds, thousands of male cicadas break into a deafening chorus. In the monsoon, it is a verdant kingdom teeming with insects, lizards, snakes, and countless other life forms as Karnala receives over 250 cm of rainfall. The breeding Whistling Thrush, Shama and White-throated Ground Thrush sing in gay abandon and are joined by croaking frogs and toads. In the east, the Patalganga River that originates in the Sahyadri is swollen by streams running off Karnala's steep rocky slopes. However, the waterfalls all but disappear soon after the monsoon. Between November and March, myriad flowering trees burst into glorious bloom, including the crimson Red Silk Cotton, and the many

The rocky pinnacle of Karnala is one of the best-known landmarks near Mumbai.

resident birds are joined by their wintering brethren – drongos, thrushes, flycatchers and leaf warblers – from the neighbouring peninsular region and the Himalaya. Although the sanctuary is not a mammal-rich area, lucky sightings of Sambar, Barking Deer and even Leopard are known to have occurred.

MORTAKA TRAIL   *From and to Mayur rest-house, c. 2 km; Mayur rest-house to NH-17, c. 1.5 km* ▶▶

In the monsoon, the tiny pond near Mayur rest-house is favoured by at least five species of amphibians such as Fungoid Frog, Indian Bull Frog and Ornate Narrow-mouthed Frog. A popular undulating trail leads along the base of the hill where, in winter, up to 40 bird species have been sighted, including Common Rosefinch. After approximately 500 m, a side trail to the left follows a steep, rocky stream-bed to Karnala Fort. The main trail traverses some fine forest of Teak, Haldu,

The Coffee Locust (top) and the female Scarlet Minivet (above) in vivid yellow plumage, add colour to the forests of Karnala.

Karanj, Kusum, Black Siris and Flame of the Forest, before turning back at a rocky stream to head towards the rest-house, or continuing along some opener terrain and scrub to the NH-17 via a small waterfall site.

FORT TRAIL   *Mayur rest-house to Karnala Fort, c. 2.5 km* ▶▶

Dense forest pervades this finest of trails. Birds are more numerous in the lower reaches, their numbers augmented by winter visitors that include Ashy Drongo, Bronzed Drongo and Verditer Flycatcher. The only sighting of the uncommon Ashy Minivet was in this area, way back in January 1965. Six birds were seen and a specimen now lies in the Bombay Natural History Society collection. Insects thrive in the monsoon when the Giant Wood Spider suspends its large intricate webs from the trees.

A panoramic view unfolds from the cliff-edge, about 1.5 km from the start of the trek. Giant industries dominate the distant landscape beyond the meandering Patalganga. The Matheran and Prabalgadh ranges stand to the northeast. The last kilometre is a trek through dense herbage, waves of grass and Karvi, where Coffee Locusts can be sighted. A rocky pinnacle rises 50 m above the windswept hilltop where the ruined fort is located. At the base of the pinnacle are water cisterns where the Malabar Whistling Thrush breeds in the monsoon. On one occasion, a pair of Eurasian Blackbird also nested here. The profusely flowering Blue Fountain Bush and some white blooms of Long-tailed Habernaria enhance the mountain scenery.

PHANSAD WILDLIFE SANCTUARY
South of Mumbai; 140 km to Supegaon gate

THE 52.72 SQ KM PHANSAD WILDLIFE SANCTUARY in the hilly country of Raigad district, lies just off the coastal Alibaug-Murud Road. This is one of the most picturesque routes around Mumbai, with the shimmering blue expanse of the Arabian Sea on one side and a dense curtain of forest on the other. Pristine sandy beaches sweep into view on the 8 km stretch from Korlai to Kashid, arguably the most scenic part of the drive.

Until 1949, when the princely Janjira state merged with the Indian Union, Phansad was the hunting reserve of its nawab. Of his many observation platforms, only Gunyachamal has escaped complete ruin.

The sanctuary harbours a sizeable population of the Indian Giant Squirrel in its thick canopy of mixed-deciduous and evergreen trees. The squirrel feeds on wild fruit and the woody Entada climber. Anjan is found in abundance in the central part of the sanctuary, this being a rare instance of the tree growing so close to the coast. *Mals*, or grasslands, break the monotony of the dense forest, allowing for sightings of the solitary Barking Deer, Sambar and small herds of Spotted Deer or Chital. The dimunitive Mouse Deer usually remains hidden from view, although Phansad is one of the better sites for viewing this elusive animal. Perennial water pools, or *gans*, in the northern narrow

The forests of Phansad are considered one of the biodiversity hotspots in the Mumbai region.

evergreen valleys have much mammal and bird activity.

Phansad hosts nearly 150 species of avifauna and offers relatively easy sightings of woodland birds such as Green Imperial Pigeon, Vernal Hanging Parakeet, Blue-faced Malkoha, Bar-winged Flycatcher-shrike and Verditer Flycatcher, which are otherwise elusive.

The walking trails are well laid from the main gate at Supegaon, facilitating exploration of the sanctuary and its wildlife. The hillier

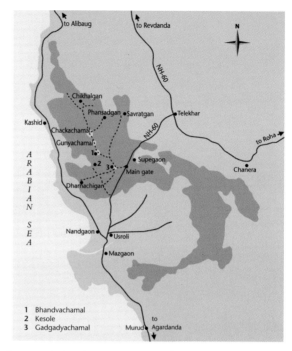

southern parts are primarily mixed-deciduous, but the following trails all lie in Phansad's northern forests of mixed-deciduous, evergreen and semi-evergreen.

CHIKHALGAN TRAIL   *Supegaon gate to Chikhalgan, 5.5 km*

Mal grasslands – Gadgadyachamal, Bhandvachamal, Gunyachamal and Chackachamal – intersperse the evergreen Anjan forest at regular intervals on this trail to Chikhalgan. The observation tower at Gadgadyachamal, about 500 m from the Supegaon gate, is a perfect vantage point, and the sight of a Mouse Deer, Barking Deer or Small Indian Civet in the wee hours of the morning more than makes up for an uncomfortable night. Densely forested Chikhalgan is ideal for observing woodland birds such as Green Imperial Pigeon, Emerald Dove, Malabar Parakeet, Grey-headed Canary

The charming Cup-n-Saucer plant gets its name from its peculiarly-shaped flowers.

Flycatcher and Honey Buzzard. The Malabar Pied Hornbill and Malabar Trogon, widespread birds in the Western Ghats are rare here, but have been reported a couple of times. At midday, the otherwise active and noisy Indian Giant Squirrel can sometimes be caught napping, its furry tail dangling against the branch of a tree.

About a kilometre after Gunyachamal, a side trail along a stream with dense evergreen forest to the right leads to Phansad Dam. It almost always offers signs of animal activity. When the monsoon abates in September and October, there is an abundance of insects, including the flashy Blue Mormon butterfly and a wealth of wondrously coloured beetles and bugs.

DHARNACHIGAN TRAIL
Supegaon gate to Dharnachigan, 3 km
This trail leads through excellent evergreen and semi-evergreen forest, another of the strongholds here of the Indian Giant Squirrel. Pugs and scat indicate the presence of Leopard, Small Indian Civet and Barking Deer. The large number of birds includes hornbills, their diminishing population finding some reprieve in this prime forest, and shy junglefowl. A diversion to the right leads to Kesole, where only the last vestiges of the summer palace of the nawab of Janjira survive amid a sprawling orchard.

SAVRATGAN TRAIL *Supegaon gate to Savratgan, c. 4 km*
The shaded pool of Savratgan is a hub of animal and bird activity, the trail cutting through semi-evergreen and evergreen forest. Sightings of the Indian Giant Squirrel are quite routine here, but the larger mammals such as Wild Boar, Spotted Deer and Barking Deer are elusive. Like much of Phansad, this is an excellent bird-watching area.

Top to bottom: The Scarlet Minivet male is very vocal during its breeding season between April and July. There is a rejuvenation of life in the monsoon months as flashy bugs mate, Fungoid Frogs abound, and mushroom clusters encrust the forest floor.

SAHYADRI HILLS

KARJAT
SE of Mumbai; 66 km to Ulhas River bridge

AWAY FROM COASTAL INFLUENCES that pervade most of the Mumbai region, Karjat, a stop on the Mumbai-Pune rail route, is a convenient base for treks to the Sahyadri Hills and the lower Matheran Range. Situated at the edge of Ulhas Valley, the surrounding sparse forest is dotted with artifical lakes, farmhouses, resorts and health spas, but several side roads lead to patches of wilderness. In the rains, the lush paddy fields as well as the verdant hills, streaked with silvery waterfalls, attract a profusion of avian visitors, many of them to breed.

ON NH-4 *Chauk junction to Halphata, c. 20 km*
The quickest route to Karjat is via the Mumbai-Pune highway (NH-4). The 10 km charming tree-lined stretch that leads off from Chauk junction to Karjat is flanked by farmhouses and nurseries. To the left is the craggy ridge of Irshal, with the Matheran massif lurking beyond. On the right, the vicinity of the small Wavarli pond teems with warblers, quails and munias in the monsoon, and some waterhen, cormorants and Little Grebes can be sighted. Winter brings with it a few waterfowl such as Pintail and Common Teal.

With the looming ridge of the Sahyadri in sight, the route from Kashele to Khandas cuts through deciduous forest sprinkled liberally with Flame of the Forest trees.

Past the pond, a bifurcation to the right to Halphata leads through a fine stretch of open scrub and light forest. The Palasdhari Lake lies en route, its name evidently derived from *palas* (Flame of the Forest) trees whose fiery orange flowers attract drongos, leafbirds and sunbirds between February and April. While there are a few waterbirds, the surrounding country is a haven for

The Spotted Dove is regularly heard and sighted in forest and along most drives here.

raptors such as Brahminy Kite, Short-toed Eagle and Booted Eagle. The area along the route is also an excellent cuckoo habitat, and as many as four species have been reported in the monsoon when these birds are highly vocal.

ALONG KARJAT-MURBAD ROAD   *Ulhas River bridge to Khandas, 28 km*
It is a picturesque drive from Karjat's Ulhas River bridge to Khandas village, the base for a popular trek up the Sahyadri Hills to Bhimashankar (1005 m). A pleasant diversion on the right, just past the Ulhas bridge at Karjat, leads to Kondavne, the base for treks to the Dhak and fort-topped Rajmachi peaks, while another diversion further on, leads to Bhivpuri tunnels.

For 10 km from the bridge to Kondavne, paddy fields intersperse open scrub in the monsoon. Light forest takes over near Kondavne. Among the mammals reported in the area are porcupine, mongoose, Striped Hyena, Jackal and the Jungle Cat, distinguished by its relatively short tail ringed with black at the end. Occasionally active by day, this feline's prey comprises small mammals, birds and even village poultry.

The diversion to the Bhivpuri Tata Power complex, at the base of the Sahyadri, occurs just over 8 km from the Ulhas River bridge. The last couple of kilometres are through deciduous forest and the bird life is fairly good, especially in the monsoon when numerous paddy fields and plentiful foliage

The Pej River slices through verdant countryside at Bhivpuri, at the base of the Sahyadri.

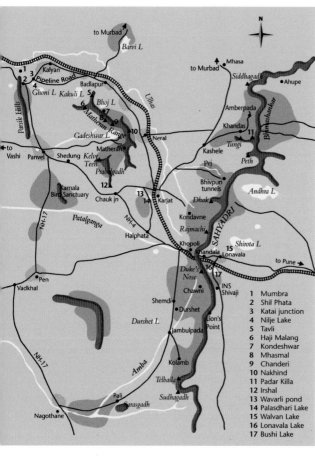

transform the parched summer landscape. With the long spur of the Dhak mountain to the right and the Pej River to the left, this is probably the most scenic stretch in the Karjat area.

At Kashele, on the Karjat-Murbad route, the road branches right to Khandas, 13 km away, and is almost entirely lined with fine deciduous forest. The Sahyadri ridge is spectacularly close and the Peth, Tungi, Bhimashankar and Siddhagadh peaks are in fine view. The Flame of the Forest is in abundance, its early summer blooms adding a splash of colour to the monotonous brown landscape, and attracting several birds and a few Common Langur. Once the Tungi ridge and the towering Bhimashankar peak close in, the forest quality improves considerably, but again opens out as Khandas approaches.

Roughly midway on the long and arduous trek from Khandas to Bhimashankar is a spectacular patch of tall evergreen forest. This is the base of Padar Killa, a rocky pinnacle from where the steep 300 m climb to Bhimashankar begins. For those who do not want a trek, the 5-km drive in sight of the towering peaks from Khandas to Amberpada, is enthralling, and sometimes affords sightings of eagles, buzzards, falcons and bands of swifts.

VASHI-KARJAT ROUTE   *Vashi toll post to Karjat junction, 80 km*
The extensive route from Vashi (Navi Mumbai) to Karjat passes a mix of habitats, from dense bamboo and shrub around Mahape all the way to the

The massive form of Bhimashankar, with Padar Killa to the right, looms over Khandas village.

rugged Matheran and Sahyadri ranges. The surrounding country is home to several reptiles, some jackal and mongoose, and the odd Striped Hyena.

The low scrub- and grass-encrusted Parsik Hills run parallel to the busy Thane-Belapur Road to its west. Near Mumbra, towards their northern fringes, are popular rock-climbing sites that until the early 1990s supported a number of Long-billed and White-rumped Vultures. Some afforestation schemes on its western slopes, notably in the Gavalideo area, have ensured the reappearance and survival of a few mammals, including jackal, hare and mongoose. Nearly 50 species of birds, including Booted Eagle, Malabar Whistling Thrush and Painted Francolin have been reported, while Python, Bronzeback Treesnake, Green Vinesnake, Checkered Keelback, Bengal Monitor and numerous other species make up the large array of reptiles.

Shil Phata is a major intersection on the old Mumbai-Pune Road east of Parsik Hills. Between Shil Phata and nearby Katai junction, shrubs such as Marsh Glory and Marsh Barbel thrive on the

The Bengal Monitor (right) was used by Maratha warriors to scale formidable forts situated on the hilltops of Sahyadri. The Gavalideo area in Parsik Hills (right above).

Small flocks of Lesser Whistling Duck (above) visit the region's numerous waterbodies at dusk. *The Oriental Skylark's (above right)* spectacular flight and song can be experienced during early summer and intermittently between October and December.

margins of the small Nilje pond in which bloom a few water lilies and lotuses. There are sightings of, not only waterside species such as Cotton Teal, Common Teal, Lesser Whistling Duck and Marsh Harrier, but occasionally a Shikra as well, as it swoops from the lakeside trees.

The MIDC Pipeline Road, east from Katai junction, traverses an open landscape of grass and scrub, offering sightings of larks, francolins, quails, shrikes, stonechats, lapwings, bee-eaters, harriers and other raptors. Early on a winter morning, close to 50 avifaunal species can be observed around the vicinity's lakes and along the varied habitats that flank this long drive.

The open, partly herbage-encrusted marsh of Ghoni, just off the MIDC Pipeline Road, not far from Nilje, is a far better birding site. Not only does it attract a few wintering species, but it has a higher concentration of resident waterside birds. Roughly 5 km east of Ghoni is Kakuli Lake, edged by tall

The Ghoni Lake attracts many birds during the rains and winter.

trees to its south and west. Its surrounding scrub and cultivation support an interesting mix of scrub and edge-of-the-forest birds. Set against the rugged backdrop of Tavli and Haji Malang, peaks of Matheran Range, Kakuli Lake is best visited in October, when the earliest of wintering waterfowl have already descended on its waters. Mammals in the vicinity include Jackal, Black-naped Hare and Common Mongoose, though none is present in any great number nor are they easily sighted.

Another diversion to the right from the Pipeline Road leads to the foot of Tavli peak, its winter hues of rich gold and brown striking against the black rock. In the monsoon, the vivid green vegetation is enveloped in thick mist. A lone Falcon and swifts whiz past the imposing pinnacles above. A route from the Pipeline Road leads left to the Barvi Lake. Partially fringed with fine mixed-deciduous forest, it has some wildlife, including the odd Leopard.

As the Pipeline Road continues southward, monsoon grass, scrub and paddy defines the open landscape on the left, while to the right the jagged peaks of the Matheran Range peep through cloud and mist. Bhoj Lake is visited by a small number of winter waterfowl. Nearby are the much-visited falls of Kondeshwar. The route continues south to provide breathtaking views of Mhasmal, Chanderi, Nakhind and other peaks

Top to bottom: *Monsoon clouds hang low over spectacular, jagged peaks; freshwater lakes such as Bhoj Lake with Badlapur Hills in the backdrop; and sprawling grass and scrub terrain along MIDC Pipeline Road – these are some of the sights along the scenic Vashi-Karjat route.*

of the Matheran Range, while Matheran itself looms above Neral. In the eastern distance are the higher peaks of the Sahyadri.

KHOPOLI-PALI ROAD
SE of Mumbai; 75 km to Pali junction

THE 40 KM KHOPOLI-PALI ROAD (SH-92) stretches along the base of the Sahyadri. Unlike the Karjat area to the north, the wide swathe of countryside south of Khopoli remains relatively untouched by farmhouse culture. The Amba River flows leisurely through the landscape to drain into Dharamtar Creek near Rewas. On the west is open, undulating scrubland, dotted with small reservoirs and paddy fields in the monsoon, contrasting with the healthy scrub and deciduous forest of the east that provides ample trekking routes to the mountains. *See map on page 54.*

SHEMDI TO CHAWNI   *4 km*
Unpaved but partly motorable, this route leads through deciduous forest along the Amba River to Chawni, at the base of Duke's Nose. Usually dry between January and June when the Yellow-wattled Lapwing has been sighted, the river swells with the monsoon rains and the surrounding herbage teems with birds and insects. From Chawni, a trek to the Lonavala-Khandala area takes up to three hours and there are pockets of evergreen jungle along the ravines where Leopard, Common Palm Civet, Wild Boar and Barking Deer still survive, though sightings are never easy.

The Amba River flows through lush country between Pali and NH-17.

DURSHET LAKE

Durshet Lake, one of the small waterbodies west of the Khopoli-Pali Road, is on a tributary of the Amba. There are fine views of the Sahyadri en route, and waterlogged paddy fields pervade the monsoon landscape. Numerous warblers, rails and crakes, and the Cinnamon Bittern converge here to breed alongside a few Jungle Bush Quail and Barred Buttonquail, an unusual species where the polyandrous female is more colourful, while the male incubates the eggs and rears the young. Post-monsoon, as the water level recedes, herons,

Cliffs and rock-faces in this stretch still harbour small breeding populations of White-rumped and Long-billed Vultures.

waterfowl and a host of open-land birds are sighted. The elusive Jungle Cat and Russell's Viper are among the wildlife reported here.

JAMBULPADA TO KOLAMB *4.5 km*

At Jambulpada, a diversion leads to Kolamb village at the base of the Sahyadri. Less spectacular than the Khandas route in Karjat, the extensive scrub and forest sustain a fair population of birds, their numbers shooting up in the monsoon and winter. The Bengal Monitor can be sighted on this route, sometimes crossing the tarred road. The route offers views of craggy peaks such as Telbaila and Sudhagadh. From Kolamb, it is a 400 m climb up the Amby Valley, the trek taking approximately three hours. Particularly delightful in the rains, when waterfalls streak down dark grey rocks, it provides sightings of Barking Deer and Common Palm Civet.

SARASGADH

The isolated rock of Sarasgadh rises to 300 m near Pali. It is believed that the fort on its summit was used as a watchtower by the great Maratha warrior, Shivaji. Surrounded by lush cultivation, scattered habitations and the low hill ranges of the Konkan, the Sahyadri can be viewed to the east. Kestrels, martins and Blue Rock Thrush are typical of this rocky terrain, and perhaps up to ten pairs of vultures, including White-rumped and Long-billed, have been recently observed breeding between January and May, sprays of white droppings marking their nesting sites. Populations of these birds have fallen considerably in recent years.

The dry river-bed of Amba in peak summer, between Shemdi and Chawni.

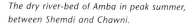

LONAVALA & KHANDALA

LONAVALA   SE of Mumbai, 95 km to Lonavala railway station
KHANDALA   SE of Mumbai, 90 km to Khandala railway station

SITUATED ATOP BHOR GHAT at the edge of the Sahyadri, on the perennially busy
Mumbai-Pune highway (NH-4), Khandala, at an altitude of about 600 m, has
become one of the most popular weekend getaways, particularly during the
monsoon when Matheran and Mahabaleshwar are practically shut off by
torrential rain. Khandala chocks up an average of 450 cm annually. Lonavala,
further east on the road, receives less rain, but swirling mists, heavy dark
clouds and howling winds make it equally magical in the monsoon.

Short drives from these bustling hill towns lead to a scenic mix of forest
and grass, with several large freshwater reservoirs. Despite spreading
urbanization, the wooded areas are filled with the melodies of Blackbird,
Malabar Whistling Thrush and the occasional Black Bulbul, while Alpine Swift
and Peregrine Falcon are seen near cliff-faces. Ryewoods, a public park in
Lonavala, has an impressive array of old trees that include Jamun, Kokam and
Indian Medlar.

A drive along the old Khandala Road passes Lonavala Lake where the
secluded southeast margin offers summer sightings of terns, plovers and larks,
some in their breeding plumage. Continuing past Bushi Lake, a popular

The higher reaches of the Sahyadri and its many narrow valleys retain some pristine evergreen forest.

tourist site during the rains, the road proceeds
through semi-evergreen and evergreen forests to
the verdant Amby Valley, passing the restricted
naval base, INS Shivaji. Primary semi-evergreen
forest and grassland on the base sustain a large
variety of birds that include Nilgiri Wood Pigeon
and Malabar Pied Hornbill. There has been an
isolated report of the Broad-tailed Grassbird. The
naval base is bordered by three lakes. Lion's Point,
4 km from INS Shivaji, offers breathtaking views
of the Konkan plains and the Khopoli-Pali Road.
The rocky crag of Tiger's Leap is seen nearby.

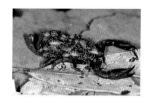

Artificial reservoirs such as Lonavala Lake,
Walvan, Shirota, Andhra (Thokerwadi), Tungarli,
Somwadi and Bushi, were created on the Lonavala–
Khandala plateau to impound water for power
generation, but have also tremendously influenced
the ecology of the area. Their water sustains rivers
such as Patalganga, Pej and Ulhas, critical for the
domestic, agricultural and industrial needs of the

A scorpion with young on its back (top), a Fox-tail Orchid (above), a Karvi-encrusted slope (below), and the spectacular drop from Lion's Point (bottom) in the Lonavala-Khandala region.

narrow Konkan belt below. They harbour a variety of waterside birds, and
during winter, a fair number of waterfowl and waders congregate here.

The Tata Power Company has done
notable work in improving the fish
population in some of these lakes.

Invigorating treks along narrow
tracks and treacherous rocky
outcrops, frequented only by falcons
and swifts, to lofty forts and
mountain tops, such as Rajmachi,
Lohagadh, Visapur and Duke's Nose,
start at Lonavala. Between August
and October, monsoon annuals –
balsams, Graham's Groundsel, Blue
Fountain Bush, Sensitive Smithia
among many others – abound in
every nook and cranny, while
waterfalls reverberate in this hilly
country. A wealth of insects and
reptiles can be observed at the
ancient rock-cut Buddhist caves of
Karla and Bhaja. *See map on page 54.*

MAHABALESHWAR
SE of Mumbai; 230 km to bus depot

THE DENSELY FORESTED HILL TOWN OF MAHABALESHWAR, in the heart of the
Sahyadri, is perhaps the most popular summer retreat near Mumbai. Famed
for its strawberry fields and panoramic views of verdant hills and valleys,
Mahabaleshwar is best visited in the dry months between October and June.
The monsoon arrives with full force in mid-June, and torrential rains and
howling winds characterize this wet season till September, when
Mahabaleshwar receives over 600 cm of rainfall.

   The first Englishman to visit Mahabaleshwar was Sir Charles Malet in
1791. In 1824, General Lodwick made the first attempts to establish a
sanatorium. At the Raja of Satara's invitation, Sir John Malcolm, governor of
Bombay, visited Mahabaleshwar in 1828, and within a year it became British
territory. The hill station was originally named Malcolm Peth after the
governor. Over the years, as the town centre developed and crops such as
potatoes and strawberries were introduced, Mahabaleshwar acquired the air of
a British country town. However, old Mahabaleshwar in the northwest, with
its ancient temples, has a very different ambience. Today, Mahabaleshwar
during the season is crammed with tourists, but thanks to a proactive

*In the last few weeks of the monsoon entire mountainsides are encrusted with flowering herbs.
A botanist's delight, Mahabaleshwar hosts almost 1000 species of plants.*

environmental lobby, it is not swamped by
hysterical development that plagues many of
India's hill towns.

With an altitude of 1372 m, the sprawling
mountain top of Mahabaleshwar covers an area of
over 130 sq km, its spurs radiating in all directions
to form viewing points that overlook low, lush
valleys as well as the surrounding flat-topped hills.
The bazaar in the town centre is the hub of all
commercial activity, and most hotels and offices are
located here. Nearby are two parks and Venna
Lake, with patches of original flora. Although
forest birds, insects, and bits of vegetation occur in
the immediate vicinity of the town centre,
Mahabaleshwar's flora and fauna is best observed
along the trails leading to its numerous points.

Armies of bulbuls and a smaller number of
babblers, flycatchers and thrushes dominate. The
Bonnet Macaque is more numerous than its black-
faced cousin, the Common Langur, and is a regular
sight at Kate's Point and Bombay Point. It is
possible to sight a Gaur or two, the closest these enormous bovines may be
seen to Mumbai, as well as Sambar, India's largest deer. The more elusive
wildlife here includes Toddy Cat and Leopard. There have been reports of
Black Panther.

*Bladderwort and bead-grass
flowers* (above) *carpet many
opens areas during September-
October. A Bonnet Macaque*
(top) *at Kate's Point.*

Windswept and rain-washed, the Anjan, Pisa, Jamun, Par Jamun and other
trees in this dense evergreen forest are rather stunted. The weeks between
mid-September and early October are the most spectacular – balsams paint
the mountains in vivid hues of purple and pink, and Common Begonias
encrust damp rocks. Gregarious flowering of Graham's Groundsel turns much
of Mahabaleshwar into
a field of yellow, as
bead-grasses,
Bladderwort, Hill
Turmeric, Arrowroot
and other flowering
plants cover both valley
and mountain. The

*Lingmala Waterfall rushing
down Venna Valley is one
of the grandest sights in
Mahabaleshwar.*

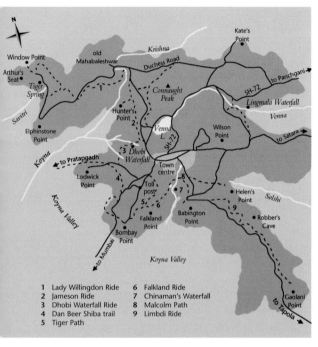

Map legend:
1 Lady Willingdon Ride
2 Jameson Ride
3 Dhobi Waterfall Ride
4 Dan Beer Shiba trail
5 Tiger Path
6 Falkland Ride
7 Chinaman's Waterfall
8 Malcolm Path
9 Limbdi Ride

Mahabaleshwar area alone boasts of over five per cent of India's flowering species.

A network of roads and trails links the town centre with the numerous viewing points. Most of the area, apart from the bridle paths, can be comfortably explored by car.

BOMBAY POINT & LODWICK POINT

These points in southwest Mahabaleshwar overlook the densely wooded Koyna Valley, and reveal stunning views of spur after spur of endless mountains and picturesque ridges and saddles. On one occasion, as many as seven Gaur have been seen grazing together. The area is home to numerous woodpeckers and the Black Eagle. This most majestic of large raptors may sometimes be observed flying low over the forest canopy in search of prey. Linking the two points is the 4 km long Dan Beer Shiba Trail, an enjoyable walk through dense, dark forests.

The Falkland Ride near Bombay Point, a trail of 5 km through dense Karvi scrub and forest, moves east along Tiger Path and Malcolm Path towards Chinaman's Waterfall and Babington Point, also accessible from the bazaar via Tapola Road. This picturesque, winding road proceeds south towards the northern fringes of Koyna Reservoir, 28 km from Mahabaleshwar.

A 2-km long bridle path near Lodwick Point leads to Dhobi Waterfall, roaring and wild in the monsoon. The path continues along a forested ridge, overlooking Koyna Valley, to meet the longer Jameson Ride that continues north along the paved road towards old Mahabaleswhar and Elphinstone Point, about 8 km from Lodwick

The Gaur in Mahabaleshwar.

Point. A short diversion to the left leads to Hunter's Point. Yet another trail near Lodwick Point heads west towards Pratapgadh Fort, 15 km away.

ELPHINSTONE POINT & ARTHUR'S SEAT

Overlooking the Koyna and Savitri Valleys, Elphinstone Point and Arthur's Seat in west Mahabaleshwar are among the most spectacular viewpoints in the Sahyadri. The drop to the plains below could be over 600 m. Falcons and Alpine Swifts soar and hunt in this wild abyss. The Krishna River to the north, an important water source of the Deccan Plateau, as well as the Savitri, Koyna, Yenna and Solshi Rivers are said to originate in the forested realm of old Mahabaleshwar and areas nearby.

The whistling calls of Puff-throated Babbler are often heard along forest trails.

About 500 m from Arthur's Seat, a bridle path descends 60 m to Tiger Spring. It is believed that many years ago, a tiger quenched its thirst here. The path joins another leading to a ledge called Window Point, with a remarkable view of deep valleys and jagged cliffs. In the monsoon, when the valleys are overgrown with foliage, thrushes sing and kestrels scream over the rocks. Near Arthur's Seat begins the Lady Willingdon Ride to old Mahabaleshwar through a wonderful 5 km of forest and scrub.

Common Kestrels in majestic flight around the jagged cliff-sides below Arthur's Seat.

Arrowroot is the dominant plant in this dense monsoon herbage covering mountain tops (above). Edible starch is made from its tubers. Strawberry cultivation has encroached upon large areas in Mahabaleshwar (top).

DUCHESS ROAD

Old Mahabaleshwar junction to Kate's Point, 4 km

The road to Kate's Point is paved but often in a state of disrepair, particularly in the monsoon. Walking is the best option. The route is through some fine evergreen forest and dense undergrowth, with intermittent pockets of strawberry fields and other farms. Near the old Mahabaleshwar junction, a short drive leading off the route reaches Connaught Peak and another long trail.

CONNAUGHT PEAK

Connaught Peak, at 1385 m, is the highest point in Mahabaleshwar after Wilson Point (1435 m) near the town centre. Cars can travel almost up to the summit, after which it is a short trek to the top. The setting is idyllic for viewing glorious sunrises and sunsets. The panoramic view encompassing Mahabaleshwar and the sprawl of verdant forest is sometimes obscured by a soft veil of morning cloud. During September and October, the rocks and clearings are carpeted with flowering plants and the cheerful yellow of Graham's Groundsel blooms.

KATE'S POINT

The terrain around Kate's Point, in north Mahabaleshwar, is rocky with plenty of dense scrub, quite distinct from the rest of forested Mahabaleshwar. Blanketing much of the open areas is the large-leaved Indian Arrowroot, a herb endemic to the Western Ghats, its showy, white flowers emerging late in the monsoon. Overlooking dense evergreen forests of the Krishna Valley in the north and the Dhom Reservoir to the east, Kate's Point is dominated by a huge rock at its edge, enhancing the view of the distant mountains and valleys. Like most other points, Kate's Point has a large number of Bonnet Macaques, with a few Common Langurs in the surrounding forest. In the monsoon, leeches infest the trails leading to the Krishna Valley.

ALONG TAPOLA ROAD

Branching off this road, the Limbdi Ride leads to Panchgani Point. Roughly 3.5 km along the ride, Robber's Cave teems with bats that include the Bearded Sheath-tailed Bat and Fulvous Fruit Bat, besides a wealth of rock-geckos, moths, spiders and scorpions.

PANCHGANI ROAD (SH-72)

The SH-72 through Mahabaleshwar leads to the smaller hill town of Panchgani, about 18 km to the east. Barely 5 km from Mahabaleshwar, evergreen forest gives way to open scrub and drier vegetation, characteristic of Panchgani that lies in the rain-shadow area. Birds typical of open country include Jungle Babbler, Indian Robin, Green Bee-eater, Pied Bush Chat and Spotted Dove, among several others. Much of the original deciduous tree cover has vanished under the combined onslaught of farmhouses, plantations, and groves of Eucalyptus and Silver Oak.

In the monsoon, Mahabaleshwar resounds with the varied calls of frogs, as brightly-coloured crabs scuttle about damp rocks.

PRATAPGADH

Pratapgadh is an hour's drive (20 km) from Mahabaleshwar, and the formidable hill fort can also be reached after a five-hour trek from Lodwick Point. Pratapgadh Fort drops steeply on some sides to reveal stunning views of the forests around. Built by the Maratha leader Shivaji in 1656, this is the historic site where he vanquished Afzal Khan of Bijapur. It is a steep walk to the fort from the car park but worth the effort.

The forests of Mahabaleshwar enveloped in mist in the monsoon.

MALSHEJ GHAT
NE of Mumbai; c. 140 km to MTDC resort

MALSHEJ GHAT (C. 850 M) IS SITUATED on the rugged 50 m long swathe from Harishchandragadh in the north to Bhimashankar in the southwest, which has an average elevation of 1000 m. Malshej, along with Naneghat, was used as a pass connecting Deccan Plateau in the east with the Konkan ports in the west.

The 11 km drive from Savarne at the base of Malshej Ghat is wildly picturesque, through jagged ridges and dense forests that harbour a fascinating wildlife, ranging from the dazzling Blue Mormon, India's largest butterfly, to elusive civets. It is an awe-inspiring 500 m drop from the Malshej plateau, and the view is spectacular. Malshej is especially enthralling in the monsoon – thick mist, dark clouds laden with moisture, tearing winds, blinding downpours, dripping rocky overhangs and waterfalls dramatically transform its landscape. Heavy verdure encrusts everything but the tarred road. The noisy croaking of frogs persists day and night, and the walls of the rest-house on the plateau top, as well as its every door and window are covered with insects, including the giant Atlas and Moon Moths and Death's Head Hawk-moths. Gaudily coloured beetles and bugs are in abundance, and snakes and lizards appear, flooded out of hidden crevices.

The Harishchandragadh mountain looms over forests en route to Malshej Ghat.

The first few weeks of the monsoon sees an influx of birds heralding their breeding season. The rest-house has become infamous as a suicide site for birds. As many as 45 species, including otherwise rarely sighted rails,

An old metal milestone (above left), one of the last vestiges of the Raj, on the Kalyan-Malshej Road. Unfortunately highways through wildernesses take an animal toll (above right).

buttonquails, crakes and cuckoos have been known to crash against the walls and glass panes, disoriented by the mist, rain, wind and lights of the rest-house. By early September, when the monsoon has subsided, swaying beds of yellow Graham's Groundsel, and pink and purple balsams begin to blanket the sprawling, mushy Malshej plateau.

Narrow foot trails explore the forest around Malshej, revealing myriad insects, frogs and birds, and the Small Indian Civet. The Barking Deer can be often heard during its rutting season in winter, and some of the other mammals in the region are Striped Hyena, Jackal and Common Langur. There is a 2.5 km walk from the rest-house to a tunnel on the main Kalyan-Junnar Road to Mumbai, but for the more intrepid, it is the arduous trek to Harishchandragadh (1491 m) that beckons, taking the better part of a day. Sporadically seen in Malshej, the Indian Giant Squirrel has regularly been sighted on this trek. Uncontrolled tourism in Malshej Ghat needs to be reviewed and managed before garbage and noise ruin this splendid site.

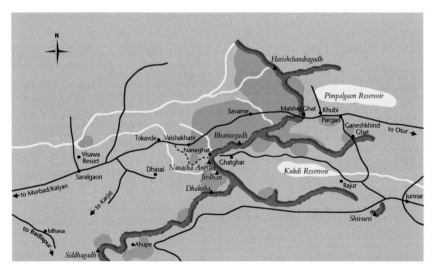

To the east of Malshej are Deccan Plateau and several reservoirs. The rambling Pimpalgaon Reservoir, formed in the late 1990s, floods in the monsoon attracting, between September and November, small flocks of the lanky Greater Flamingo with other aquatic birds such as herons and cormorants. Migratory waterfowl in winter include Red-crested Pochard, Pintail, Garganey and Shoveller.

In summer, the dry open lands and small islands draw a few terns and Little Ringed Plover. A May sighting of a Kentish Plover pair in breeding plumage and the Indian Skimmer with its prominent orange bill has been recorded. The open scrub area around the reservoir is ideal for chats, larks, shrikes, doves, kestrels and Black-shouldered Kite. The reservoir is certainly influencing the ecology of the region, with a spate of aquatic flora and fauna, including numerous fish, prawns and crabs, invading this vast new habitat.

NANEGHAT   *East of Mumbai; c. 105 km to Vaishakhare*

Naneghat was a vital link between Junnar, the capital of the erstwhile Satvahana dynasty, and the busy ports of Kalyan and Nalla Sopara. Although the highly popular trek to this 830 m high hilltop starts at Vaishakhare, it is possible to drive all 189 km from Mumbai to Naneghat. The road is circuitous and little known via Malshej, while the trek takes only four or five hours. From the base can be viewed the peculiar form of Nanacha Angtha on one side of Naneghat, as well as Jivdhan, Vanarlingi and Dhakoba peaks.

The 5 km trek through a well-laid path is primarily along tall forest. Somewhat stunted in the windswept upper slopes, the trees give way to open scrub in the higher reaches. The forest is alive with the calls of barbets, drongos, leafbirds, orioles, tree-pies, bulbuls and woodpeckers, particularly when the Flame of the Forest and Red Silk Cotton are in bloom between January and March. However, most hikers prefer the monsoon beauty of late June to October.

The last bit of the climb is through a rocky canyon, fringed by ancient caves, jagged rock-cut steps and water cisterns. A huge stone jar marks the end of the trek. It is believed that it was used to collect toll from traders, and receives coins even today from passers-by. The mountain top opens on to a

A Yellow-legged Buttonquail disoriented in the monsoon nights (above). *For weeks in the misty, wet monsoon, every wall in the Malshej rest-house is encrusted with moths, such as the Moon Moth* (top).

plateau with cactus-like vegetation and a carpet of golden grass that contrasts vividly with the dark rocks. At this height, the fast-flying Alpine Swift and raptors such as Common Kestrel and Peregrine Falcon are regularly sighted, the trisyllabic whistle of a soaring Crested Serpent Eagle resounding through the air. The Indian Giant Squirrel

The sprawling Pimpalgaon Reservoir is fast changing the ecology around Malshej Ghat.

has also been sighted here. The higher, fort-topped Jivdhan (1126 m), treacherous Vanarlingi, thumb-like Nanacha Angtha, and a series of other peaks are seen, offering one of the most spectacular views in the area.

MALSHEJ GHAT TO NANEGHAT TOP BY ROAD   *54 km*

It is a back-breaking drive on a winding and, occasionally, non-existent road to almost the top of Naneghat. Eleven kilometres east of Malshej, at Pargao, the forests dissipate into scrub and light plantations. Ganeshkhind Ghat lies en route, and Shivneri (1003 m) dominates the eastern skyline. Grass and scrub birds such as Sirkeer Malkoha and small noisy bands of Large Grey Babbler have been sighted. After reaching the Naneghat valley, much of the drive is along Kukdi (Manikdoh) Reservoir, surrounded by open scrub. Spectacular cliff-sides are the refuge of small nesting colonies of the mysteriously diminishing Long-billed Vulture. A few caves and sparse habitation dot the light scrub and forest, ideal for chats, babblers, doves, bee-eaters, buntings and larks. The black-and-brown Crested Bunting has been observed breeding between May and August, when its long drawn-out melodious song is heard.

After nearly 44 km, Jivdhan peak stands out prominently, and the conspicuous rock of Nanacha Angtha, resembling a huge, resting frog, surveys the valley. A little later, near Ghatghar, the massive basalt pillar of Vanarlingi comes into view. The road from Ghatghar offers arguably one of the most spectacular views in the Sahyadri and terminates at the very rock of Nanacha Angtha, near the stone jar. The 100 m trek to the top is tiring but worth the awe-inspiring panorama of the plains below. The striking western rock-face of Jivdhan and a range of taller peaks towards the south form part of the view, as does Bhairavgadh peak in the north.

BHIMASHANKAR
NE of Mumbai; c. 240 km to MTDC guest-house

THE INDIAN GIANT SQUIRREL, an agile, furry-tailed animal, is locally referred to as *shekru*. Easily alarmed, its large leaf-and-stick nest tucked high up a tree is easier to sight than the animal itself, though its raucous cry is often heard. This shy animal has played a major role in having Bhimashankar declared a wildlife sanctuary.

A six-hour drive from Mumbai, Bhimashankar looms directly over Khandas village near Karjat, and boasts one of the twelve *jyotirlingas* dedicated to Lord Shiva. The sanctuary forests spreads over 130.78 sq km and is well preserved. The rains are heavy, averaging almost 500 cm, and much of the terrain is covered with moist evergreen forest, tall and dense with lush undergrowth in the valleys and along stream-beds, but stunted on the exposed crests and cliffs. Rock-strewn grassy sites are also seen on the ridges, while the slopes are carpeted with dense Karvi bushes.

A couple of years ago, a tiger was reportedly seen here, but there has been no report since. There are chances of coming across Leopard and Small Indian Civet. The forest is also home to the rarely seen scaly Indian Pangolin. It emerges from its burrow to feed at night on ants and termites. When probed, it curls up into a tight ball. There is a variety of birds – hornbills, including

The vista from Nagphani Point is among the grandest in the Sahyadri.

the Malabar Grey, woodpeckers, parakeets, bulbuls, orioles, babblers, flycatchers such as the Ultramarine and White-bellied Blue, and the Green Imperial Pigeon. The wary Grey Junglefowl is more often heard than seen. Among the bird rarities reported here are Black-crested Baza, usually restricted to the southern Western Ghats, and Fairy Bluebird.

During summer and soon after the monsoon, flitting butterflies include the peculiarly patterned Map Butterfly that is sometimes seen mud-peddling on the drying stream-beds. Giant moths, beetles, praying mantis, grasshoppers and bugs swarm the forest during the rains, luring spiders, lizards and snakes.

The sanctuary area includes the wooded Bhima and Ghod river valleys, the dense forests of Kondhawal and Ahupe, and some *adivasi* tribal hamlets. However, the infrastructure remains woefully inadequate to meet the demands of the temple-visiting crowds, and problems beset this splendid wilderness. *See map on page 54.*

KHANDAS–BHIMASHANKAR TREK

Khandas to Bhimashankar Temple, c. 5 km ▶▶

There are two routes from Khandas to Bhimashankar Temple – the Sidhi Ghat or Ladder Route, steep and via Koli, a village 3 km from the temple, and the Ganeshkhind route. At two sites en route to Koli, iron ladders affixed to the rock somewhat ease the climb. The second, easier trek is up to five hours long, with the excellent forest midway filled with birds and a possibility of seeing a sneaking Small Indian Civet by day. The Malabar and Bamboo Pit Vipers emerge in the monsoon.

Top to bottom: *The dense forests of Bhimashankar harbour a bewitching array of life forms – the Map Butterfly, Bamboo Pit Viper, Catleg Spider and bioluminiscent fungus.*

GUPT-BHIMASHANKAR TRAIL

Bhimashankar Temple to Bhorgiri, c. 4 km ▶▶

For a while, this walk through dense tree cover and luxuriant undergrowth runs parallel to a stream. Shiny black and highly gregarious Whirligig Beetles dash about in its shaded pools. Nearby, a *shivling* (a phallic symbol representing Lord Shiva) and a Nandi bull statue mark the site where the Bhima River is said to gush forth.

Along the trail, expect sightings of Indian Giant Squirrel, Malabar Grey Hornbill, White-bellied Blue Flycatcher, Black and Yellow-browed Bulbuls, Malabar Parakeet and Nilgiri Wood Pigeon. Pugs and scat along the trail betray the presence of Barking Deer, Mouse Deer, Sambar, Wild Boar and civets. The trail continues down towards Bhorgiri village and a small dilapidated fort.

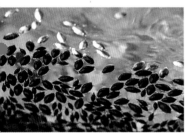

NAGPHANI TRAIL

MTDC resort to Nagphani Point, c. 2 km ▶▶

Nagphani Point (*c.* 1000 m) is the highest in Bhimashankar and is thought to resemble a hooded cobra from the plains. This trek traverses open scrub and then forest to reach the upper plateau near the hilltop, open and grassy, with panoramic views of the Padar Killa, Peth, Dhak, Siddhagadh and Gorakhgadh peaks. This is among the finest spots to see Peregrine Falcon, Common Kestrel, Honey Buzzard and Alpine Swift, and there is always the possibility of sighting some eagles and vultures.

A short trail of about 1.6 km, from the MTDC resort to a watchtower, runs through open scrub and rock, edged with tall evergreen forests and displays signs of leopard movement and Barking Deer. This is excellent habitat for nightjars and Black-naped Hare.

Top to bottom: *The Gupt-Bhimashankar trail through dense, tall forest. On secluded streams, Whirligig Beetles swirl about. The Bhimashankar Temple draws many devotees.*

SCRUB & GRASS

AAREY MILK COLONY
North Mumbai; 21 km to main gate

Heralding the dawn of the Mumbai milk supply scheme in 1949, the government acquired nearly 1600 ha of land covered by secondary growth and forest on Salsette island, north of Bombay, to set up the Aarey milk cooperative. The entire jungle was cleared to plant several species of grasses to nurture livestock. *Para* or Mauritius grass, introduced in the mid-1890s from South Africa, today covers a large area of Aarey Milk Colony.

Lying towards the southwest fringes of Sanjay Gandhi National Park, Aarey is the largest open area in Mumbai. The busy Aarey Road runs through it for 6 km, connecting the western suburbs to Powai Lake and Mumbai's eastern suburbs. The few low hills dotting the landscape retain some of the original deciduous flora. Contiguous to the national park, Aarey must have had, at one time, a similar biodiversity composition. However, over the years, grass cultivation, with intermittent scrub and introduced tree cover, has greatly influenced its ecology, even attracting a wealth of insects that in turn lure a host of predators, mostly birds. Nearly 50 kinds of butterflies and at least seven species of praying mantis have been observed here, while of the profusion of grasshoppers, most numerous are the short-horned variety,

The grass and scrub vegetation of Aarey, the largest open stretch in Mumbai, is a medley of original and introduced flora.

recognized by their short antennae and ovipositor, an organ at the tip of the abdomen through which the female deposits her eggs. The long-horned grasshoppers, popularly called Katydids, prefer dense herbage and shrub.

The mauve, crinkled flowers of the Queen's Flower tree appear during summer.

Aarey's typical grass and scrub avifauna includes bulbuls, quails, doves, bee-eaters, drongos and warblers, of which the prinias are fairly common. Four varieties, including the closely related Common Tailorbird, breed here, sometimes all year through, given the abundant grass and herbage. Forest birds of some lightly wooded patches include flycatchers and the occasional Orange-headed Ground Thrush and Red Spurfowl. An impressive 126 bird species have been recorded in Aarey.

A few mammals spill over from the main park area, but hardly any have established a good hold. The Leopard is regularly sighted around scattered pockets of habitation and cattle sheds, evidently in search of easy prey. It hunts pariah dogs and has been occasionally observed scavenging on dead livestock. The once widespread Striped Hyena probably no longer exists; two were

The Leopard is a frequent sight around the scattered habitation and cattle sheds of Aarey.

Top to bottom: *Aarey is home to a wealth of species, which includes Hooded Grasshopper, Peacock Pansy and the noisy, wintering Long-tailed Shrike. The small seasonal pond in Aarey teems with insects, amphibians and birds during the monsoon.*

found dead on the Aarey-national park border in the early 1990s, possibly persecuted by humans. Encounters with mongoose, jackal and Common Palm Civet are few, and a small number of Wild Boar exist close to the park's edge. The comfortable trails in Aarey are especially marvellous for nature-watching in the latter half of the monsoon. *See map on page 20.*

CHOTA KASHMIR

A short walk in the landscaped garden opposite Chota Kashmir Boat Club reveals some fine specimens of Traveller's Palm and Fish Tail Palm, while a few lofty cacti enhance the scenery. Ashoka, Queen's Flower and Bottle-brush trees, as well as numerous Karaya grow in this neighbourhood. The garden is a good spot for photographing butterflies of which nearly 20 kinds have been sighted. Together with the surrounding area, it hosts a number of edge-of-forest, scrub and grass birds.

NEW ZEALAND HOSTEL TRAIL

Aarey gate to New Zealand Hostel junction, 3.5 km (via New Zealand Hostel) ▶▶

A walk or drive on the paved path off the main Aarey Road leads to New Zealand Hostel. The grass and scrub along this path are ideal for warblers, shrikes, drongos, quails and a few raptors, including the occasional *Aquila* eagle. The landscape around the hostel has more tree cover and the road to the small seasonal pond, close to the junction of Aarey and Hostel Roads, has a profusion of Bonfire Trees, a beautiful sight when they flower in March and April. The abundance of monsoon flora includes Spiral Ginger and Glory Lily, an annual climber with one of the most flamboyant flowers in the region.

The pond is overgrown with herbage during the monsoon and is an excellent site for observing insects and birds between June and November. Waterside birds such as Lesser Whistling Duck,

Little Grebe (which dives underwater for fish), White-breasted Waterhen and occasional Bronze-winged and Pheasant-tailed Jacanas, have been seen breeding and accompanied by chicks in August-September. These birds vanish when the pond dries up by early summer. The surrounding scrub and secondary growth have a good selection of birds typical of such habitat and Common Mongoose and Bengal Monitor are sighted now and then.

The orange-red flowers of the Bonfire Tree appear in dense clusters during early summer.

MODERN BAKERY TRAIL   *Modern Bakery junction to pond, c. 2 km* ▶▶

An abundance of trees, including endemic varieties such as Bonfire Tree and Red Silk Cotton, and exotic species that include Flamboyant (Gulmohar) and Copper Pod, line this circuitous trail to the seasonal pond. There are some patches of dense scrub in this largely edge-of-Aarey terrain. The Leopard is a frequent visitor to the area, attracted by pariah dogs, cattle and human habitations. The scrub and verdure past the various technical units of Aarey is fine habitat for scrub birds such as bulbuls, doves, drongos, quails and babblers. Small bands of White-throated Babblers are usually easier to sight in this open scrub area. The Pied Cuckoo, a monsoon breeding visitor to the region, can be both heard and seen, occasionally chased by House Crows.

The Spiral Ginger flowers in Aarey's dense foliage of herbs in the monsoon.

ALL INDIA RADIO STATION

North Mumbai; 26 km to gate. Permission required from administrative office on site

BARELY 150 M PAST A SMALL FRESHWATER POND, and Bageecha Restaurant on the Marve Road, is an inconspicuous gate on the left, almost lost amid bush growth. This is the entrance to the sprawling 100 ha AIR station at Malvani, one of the few large sites in Mumbai to have retained some of its original creek-edge flora and fauna.

A restricted area overgrown with grass, dense scrub and a myriad trees, it is edged by some private estates, and mango and *chiku* orchards. The north-eastern fringes of Malad Creek flank the site to its west. From the gate, a narrow, paved road, extending 1.6 km south, serves as a surprisingly fine nature walk. In the rains, a variety of annuals, herbs and shrubs carpet the AIR grounds.

The towering transmission towers and cables serve as perches for raptors, including the occasional Steppe and Imperial Eagles. There are also chances of viewing a few harriers gliding low over grass and scrub to hunt small birds, rodents, lizards and insects. The Pied Harrier, a highly uncommon bird in this part of the country, was sighted here in March 2003. Among other infrequent birds reported are Barred Buttonquail, Laughing Dove and, unusual for the Mumbai region, Common Babbler.

Dense grass and herbage characterizes much of AIR station's landscape.

Open grass and scrub are also an ideal habitat for snakes such as Common Krait, which can grow to up to 1.2 m. Rarely sighted by day, when it hides in crevices and under rocks, this famed, venomous snake feeds on frogs, rodents and smaller snakes such as Wolf Snake and Banded Racer. Also found are Russell's Viper, Spectacled Cobra, Common Kukri and numerous keelbacks.

The Common Mongoose might be seen darting across the road, and also the Bengal Monitor. What is most certainly sighted is the Jackal. Although in many areas, the Jackal emerges from its burrow around dusk to feed at night, here it may be commonly sighted by day, sometimes very close to people and vehicles. They greatly relish the fruit of Indian Jujube or *ber* tree which is normally plentiful in such habitats. Creek-sides and surrounding scrubland have become the last stronghold of the Jackal in the Mumbai region. The Jungle Cat, a species that appears to be on the decline in the region, has been also seen here. *See map on page 91.*

Top to bottom: *The Indian Silverbill sometimes makes its home in an old Baya nesting colony. A jackal ambles across the AIR station grounds in broad daylight as a young Russell's Viper slithers in the herbage.*

TALZAN
NW Mumbai; 30 km to Talzan hillock

BEFORE THE CHARKOP AND GORAI developments of the early 1980s, much of the area east of Manori Creek was mangrove and salt-pan land, teeming with larks, curlews and other waders. Now only Talzan, an area of about 75 ha, remains semi-wild, though under imminent threat of urbanization when the Coastal Regulation Zone rules are relaxed.

The low hillock of Talzan on the creek's eastern fringe is densely covered by lush palms and evergreens, such as Black Plum (*jamun*), Mango and Karanj. A large variety of birds seek refuge here, and several waterside species flock to the seasonal ponds to the south, which become dry by early summer. Off the main arterial road is a network of short side roads, created as part of the area's development in the late 1980s, but now overgrown with foliage. These side roads lead to the hillock through a landscape dominated by grass, scrub and patches of stunted mangrove, and afford incredibly easy sightings of birds. This area turns a luxuriant green in the monsoon and, amid copious grass growth, plentiful varieties of wild flowers magically appear, including Glory Lily, Oriental Sesame, Devil's Claw, Brazil Jute, Common Balsam, Butterfly Bean, Passion Flower and Touch Me Not, supporting over 40 species of butterflies so far reported, including Great Eggfly, Crimson Rose and Blue Pansy.

A rain-filled depression flanked by the luxuriant vegetation of the low Talzan hillock.

During August and September, a few Tussar Silk Moths are sighted on Indian Jujube (*ber*) trees or in the surrounding herbage, as gaudily coloured Blister Beetles and Ladybirds munch feverishly on the foliage. The profusion of insects gives Talzan a bird tally of 131 species. A small flock of Lesser Kestrel was sighted in November 2001, evidently the only recent record of the species in the Mumbai region.

The Tussar Silk Moth rests in herbage by day (above).
The secretive White-breasted Waterhen resolutely holds on to a few sites in Mumbai (top).

In April, large congregations of Grey Wagtail, Yellow Wagtail and Rosy Starling are common. There is an abundance of resident warblers, notably Plain Prinia and Ashy Prinia, in the monsoon. At this time, the small population of the secretive Yellow-eyed Babbler, a by and large diminishing species in the Mumbai region, is in its breeding season and highly vocal.

Except for a few Jackal, Common Mongoose, the odd Jungle Cat and numerous rodents, mammals are scarce. Fourteen species of reptiles and four amphibians, including very large Common Bull Frogs, have been observed. *See map on page 96.*

Introduced long ago as a fibre plant from Brazil, the Brazil Jute has invaded most open sites and become among the most widespread flora.

PANVEL

East of Mumbai; 35 km to Panvel pond; 52 km to Gadeshwar Lake

OVER THE LAST TWO DECADES, Panvel, on the Mumbai-Pune route (NH-4), has witnessed rapid industrial and construction growth, robbing the area of much of its open landscape and original flora. However, bits of wilderness miraculously survive. The hills of Matheran are not too far east.

A kilometre short of Panvel, a large pond to the right is partially hidden by a dense edging of reeds. Overgrown with lotuses, water lilies, bulrushes and marsh glories (*Ipomoea*), large congregations of Lesser Whistling Duck frequent the pond that also attracts a few wintering waterfowl such as Northern Pintail, Common Teal, Garganey and perhaps even the occasional Shoveller. The 100 m open stretch of the pond along Panvel Cultural Centre and Dr Kale Hospital is an ideal place for observing birds, and the Great Cormorant, a large fish-catching, glossy black bird, has been seen here.

The sizeable Gadeshwar Lake, set prettily against the Matheran Range, is close to Panvel. En route to the lake, the enormous Chanderi peak looms to left and the Prabalgadh masiff with its pinnacle of Kelve Teen is seen on the right. A diversion on the way leads to another large waterbody. The Morbe Reservoir has the Badlapur Hills, a part of the Matheran Range, as a backdrop. The Gadeshwar Lake area is enchanting in the monsoon when it is

The scenic Gadhi River en route to Gadeshwar Lake.

carpeted with paddy fields, marshes and annuals in bloom. Numerous birds, such as Cinnamon Bittern and Painted Snipe, are well into their breeding season. Asian Openbill, Glossy Ibis and Black-headed Ibis can be seen, and the Comb Duck has been sighted in early August. The hills nearby are shrouded in cloud while numerous monsoonal insects are on display in the surrounding scrub and secondary growth.

Butterflies are seen in late September and most of October, when migratory waterfowl also arrive. The countryside is home to Jackal, Common Mongoose and Toddy Cat. A short distance from Gadeshwar Lake is Dudhani village, the starting point for treks to Matheran as well as to Peb (474 m) and its hill-fort. *See map on page 54.*

The Bronze-winged Jacana (above right) is one of several waterbirds that visit the Panvel pond (below). The gregarious Silver Spiked Cockscomb blooms towards the end of monsoon (top).

Bassein Fort & Naigon
North of Mumbai; 64 km to fort

NORTH OF BASSEIN CREEK lie the splendid ruins of a fort that was occupied by the Portuguese in 1534. They built a magnificent city around it, and Bassein (Vasai) soon gained fame as the Portuguese capital of north Konkan. In 1739, the Marathas gained control of the fort, and when Bassein became part of the Bombay Presidency in the early 19th century, the fort passed into British hands. The fortified city was neglected and nature crept back into this huge abandoned settlement.

The area around the fort is a veritable forest of trees – Date Palm, Mango, Tamarind and ficus – amid plentiful shrubbery, creepers and climbers. The ancient Baobab trees, with a huge girth that narrows to the top, were apparently introduced by the Portuguese from Africa.

The high fort walls provide a spectacular view of Bassein Creek to the south, the domain of terns, gulls and numerous waders. The ruins teem with aestivating toads and frogs, rock geckos, spiders and scorpions. The Jackal usually emerges at dusk, when it is possible to catch a glimpse of this secretive animal or, perhaps, hear its howls. The Brown Fish Owl has been reported in the vicinity. *See map on page 18.*

A dense foliage of trees, shrubs, creepers and climbers encrusts the ruins of the once magnificent Bassein Fort, occupied by the Portuguese in the 16th century.

NAIGON ROUTE

Juichandar junction (NH-8) to Tivri, 10 km ▶▶

The Naigon route is the recommended approach to Bassein Fort, more interesting than the direct road from Sativali junction. The extensive grass and scrub vegetation around Juichandar junction remains one of the finest lark habitats, although these birds have almost disappeared from Mumbai city. Four species of larks, including Rufous-tailed and Malabar-crested have been observed breeding here in the summer months.

The rains transform Juichandar's open lands into extensive grassy sprawls or waterlogged paddy fields and a host of other birds take over, from elusive bitterns and rails to tiny, delirious warblers. Frogs abound, and the large non-venomous Rat Snake is

Spiders (above) *and geckos* (top) *in dark corners and crevices of the fort.*

quite common. Marsh Harrier and Black-shouldered Kite can be seen towards the end of the monsoon.

About 1.5 km from the junction is the small Bapane Reservoir, worth a few scrub and aquatic birds, sometimes including raptors such as the occasional *Aquila* eagle. Some waterfowl may appear in winter and monsoon months. Along the road to Vasai, grass and scrub yield to extensive marshes, teeming with fish, crab and perhaps other marine life, which partly sustain the local communities who employ traditional fishing methods. In winter, fairly large congregations of waders are possible and sometimes include Curlew Sandpiper. Imperial Eagle, Short-toed Eagle and Common Kestrel are some of the raptors sighted along this route. The stretch beyond Tivri is much disturbed by quarrying and stone-crushing activities.

BASSEIN FORT AREA   *Chimaji Appa statue to fort jetty, 1.2 km* ▶▶

Opposite the statue of Chimaji Appa – the Maratha warrior who overthrew the Portuguese in Bassein in 1739 – is a narrow road, paved for the first 300 m, along the fort ramparts leading to Saint Gonsalo Garcia School. Near the school, it is possible to gain access to the entire overgrown fort complex. The virtual forest of date palm, tamarind and mango rings with the shrill cries of palm squirrels and numerous birds. The small, highly venomous Saw-

scaled Viper can sometimes be seen basking on a rock as several geckos, silent and sharp-eyed, lurk in dark corners.

The trail continues towards the jetty, offering sightings of Greater Coucal, Alexandrine Parakeet, Black-rumped Flameback, Paradise Flycatcher and White-throated Fantail, among others. Near the jetty is a small restaurant, as well as some boabab trees. From the jetty, a short 500 m road along the fort's ramparts reaches back to the statue.

The White-throated Kingfisher's melodious song is heard during March-June (left). The Brahminy Kite is an easily sighted waterside raptor (top). The open marsh and grass along the Naigon route is a birdwatcher's delight (below).

COAST & WETLAND

MALAD CREEK
NW Mumbai; 20 km to BMC Versova Lagoon, 25 km to Marve junction, 34 km to Madh jetty

DEVELOPMENTAL DEMANDS particularly threaten Malad Creek. Over 200 ha of pristine mangroves were recently cleared along its eastern margin for a golf course project, a travesty of environmental protection laws. The stretch from Bangur Nagar to Marve Road, along the creek's eastern margin, once teemed with waders and terns.

Although a large patch of mangrove survives in the creek's central areas, the healthier tracts, dominated by White Mangrove, lie on its western fringe. This widespread mangrove can attain a height of 6 m in areas well flushed by tides. Jackal and Common Mongoose are sighted even today in the mangrove and surrounding scrub, especially along Lokhandwala Back Road, where dense mangroves are edged with Castor Oil Plant, Christ's Thorn and Brazil Jute, among other creek-edge vegetation. The Jungle Cat, once widespread, is rarely sighted along the creek's eastern length, but the loud cries of Clamorous Reed Warblers are audible even from a distance. The creek is favoured by many wintering birds, while numerous heronries are located on tall trees along its eastern fringes.

The creek's eastern side is approachable from Lokhandwala Back Road while the Marve and Madh Roads provide access to its western fringe.

Mangroves, BMC Versova Lagoon, and a proposed golf site on the eastern margin of Malad Creek.

BMC VERSOVA LAGOON

Permission required from site office

Birds teem around this 26-ha sewage treatment plant, its artificial lagoons and narrow, paved roads. The Lesser Whistling Duck and Brahminy Kite are often seen. There is a dense roadside growth of Toothbrush Plant and the unusually resolute vine, White Day Glory, both swarming with insects that attract several wintering warblers and a few Bluethroat. Jackals are often encountered by night in the light tree growth on the eastern edge, frequently also appearing on the Back Road, but they are more commonly seen on Dharivali Tekdi, a hillock across Malad Creek to the west, visible from the lagoon.

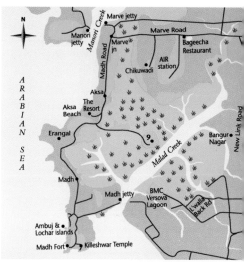

The labyrinth of channels in the creek sustains a wealth of life-forms in its nutrient-rich ooze.

The flowers of the gregarious Sea Holly add colour to the creek-side (above). A nesting Indian Pond Heron (top).

MADH ROAD   *Marve junction to Madh jetty, 9 km*

The 9-km stretch from Marve junction to Madh jetty traverses a narrow coastal strip, the scrub area dotted with Tamarind and Toddy Palm as well as interspersing groves of coconut, *chiku*, mango and cashewnut. Rock and sand alternate along this delightful coastline, host to old villages, modern bungalows and upmarket resorts.

The wide eastern strip of grass and scrub after Marve junction extends 1.5 km to Aksa village. Ideal for open-land birds, Red-wattled Lapwing, Spotted Dove, Indian Robin and even a few larks such as Oriental Skylark have been seen here, and in the early 1980s the Oriental Pratincole was reported in a rare sighting for the Mumbai region. There is a fair chance of spotting Jackal and Common Mongoose. In the monsoon, numerous warblers and occasional Jungle Bush Quail and Barred Buttonquail may be seen.

A short diversion from the tree-lined Madh Road leads to Aksa beach, crowded over weekends, but between October and early April, sprinkled with gulls, terns and waders. A few flamingos were sighted in 2000 and 2001. Beyond the turning to Aksa and the sight of Dharivali Tekdi looming above the stunted mangroves to the east, the road branches towards a rocky coastline where the elusive Yellow-wattled Lapwing was seen in the 1980s and early 1990s.

The main route progresses towards Erangal and Madh, largely inhabited by fishing communities. Monsoon rarities include Masked Booby, a large pelagic bird that blows in on monsoon winds. At Madh, a narrow road leads to Lochar and Patwadi fishing jetties from where the small, rocky islets of Ambuj and Lochar can be reached by boat. Waders congregate here in early summer, prior to emigration. Evidently, a small population of Little Tern once bred on Lochar as on Uttan-Vashi islet, further north.

The last diversion off Madh Road leads to Killeshwar Temple as well as the small Madh Fort, built by the Portuguese and now overgrown with foliage, the area around covered by dense scrub and trees. In winter, the impressive Peregrine Falcon is sometimes seen on its ramparts and the large White-bellied Sea Eagle was once reported. About 20 bird species can be sighted in this area, including White-throated Fantail, Greater Coucal and Golden Oriole. Terns, hoopoes and stonechats sometimes frequent the fish-drying yard near the temple. In 2002, a possible record count of 64 House Crow nests was made on the huge Pipal tree nearby.

TO DHARIVALI TEKDI   *Aksa beach turning to Dharivali Tekdi, 2.5 km* ▶▶

A dirt-track leads east off Madh Road to Dharivali Tekdi, about 150 m past the Aksa beach turning, along scrub, stunted mangroves and salt-flats. Waders may congregate here in late March and April, several in breeding plumage prior to emigration. The Yellow-wattled Lapwing, somewhat rare in the region, was sighted till the early-1990s. A fish-drying yard to the left is usually crammed with cattle egrets, terns and gulls in winter. The Toothbrush Plant and Sea Holly are among the mangrove-associated plants seen en route. Dharivali Tekdi rises above the dense mango and other tree cover, its top affording spectacular views of Malad Creek. Here, Jackal is often seen easily by day, and its signs are frequent. The Jungle Cat, too, has been sighted.

Dharivali Tekdi, with its light scrub, and groves along its base is an ideal habitat for jackals.

The area around Madh Fort, an interesting combination of sea, creek and verdure, is a rewarding birdwatch site.

MANORI CREEK, GORAI & UTTAN
NW Mumbai; 26 km to Marve jetty, 32 km to Borivli jetty

MUCH OF MANORI CREEK'S eastern fringe of mangroves has been encroached upon, while refuse chokes some of the rest. Even so, well over 50 species of birds have been reported. The reeking Gorai landfill site, just off Borivli jetty, teems with birds, mostly wagtails, egrets, rosy starlings and innumerable raptors, including *Aquila* eagles.

The eastern mud-flats can be observed from the jetty. Low tide brings a fair sprinkling of waders, some mudskippers and other marine creatures, including some fiddler crabs, waving outsized claws in their mating ritual. A few terns, kingfishers and cormorants perch on fishing poles, a probable site for the colourful Black-capped Kingfisher, though the large Caspian Tern, with its distinctive red bill, is becoming increasingly rare.

To the west of the creek are mangroves and a mix of salt-flats, scrub and rock. The 10 km coastal stretch from Manori to Uttan offers a medley of habitats – sandy beaches, rocky coast, open scrub and low hills, interspersed with dense groves, plantations and ample Palmyras. Interesting bird sightings include the highly uncommon Crab Plover on Gorai beach. Though a widespread winter visitor, the region's only recorded nesting site of the Paradise Flycatcher was also in Gorai.

Flowers of the Indian Coral add colour to the Palmyra-dotted coastal stretch of Manori-Gorai.

KANDARPADA TRAIL

Bhakti Complex police booth to dense mangroves, c. 1.5 km ▶▶

About 250 m of this fine walk along the eastern margins of the creek is paved, and the rest is a dirt-track through mangroves fringed by associate plants such as Shore Purselane and Mangrove Beanstalk. Jackals form a healthy population and may be sighted by day, while pugs of the elusive Jungle Cat are occasionally spotted. Winter migrants include Bluethroat and warblers, the bird tally easily reaching 35 species in two hours. The largely nocturnal Eurasian Thick-knee, uncommon in the Mumbai region, has been seen once. Interestingly, a Peregrine Falcon, sometimes with a mate, has been a regular winter visitor since late 1999, seen settled on transmission towers or charging at waders and pigeons. A courting Bengal Monitor may be encountered on the trail in early winter.

The Golden Oriole is one of the several arboreal birds regularly sighted in this region.

TO CULVEM   *Manori jetty to Culvem, 4 km*

The short ferry ride from Marve to Manori jetty transports one to a world very different from crowded, built-up Mumbai. The largely open scrub and Toddy Palms along the trail were once home to Ashy Wood Swallows that have now almost vanished from Mumbai. The sparse cover around the temple sites near the jetty includes Bonfire Tree, its flowers attracting a few birds in March–April. In the monsoon, prinias, Zitting Cisticolas and cuckoos are seen along with a few quails and Yellow-eyed Babbler. Some waders and herons frequent the stretch of stunted mangroves at low tide. The fish-drying area now sees dismally few Whiskered and Gull-billed Terns. The Manoribel and Dominica Hotels, spread over almost 5 ha, are recommended stopovers for watching sunbirds, bulbuls, ioras, flycatchers, drongos and warblers. A pair of Grey Hornbills was sighted in 2002. In the monsoon, paddy fields and a profuse burst of annuals dramatically transform the landscape around.

The bird-rich groves and private estates in the area.

Map labels:

to Vasai
Panju
N
Bassein Fort
Bassein Creek
Dongri Dhakka
Uttan Bhayandar Road
Bhayandar
Uttan-Vashi
Uttan
Dongri
A R A B I A N   S E A
Bhaiti
Uttan jn
Mira Bhayandar Road
Maxwell Hotel
3
Dahisar quarry
Western Express Highway
Orchard   1
Dahisar
Gorai jn
Gorai Jetty Road
Borivli jetty   2
Gorai bus depot
Esselworld
Gorai jetty
Gorai Link Road
LT Road
Culvem
Borivli
SV Road
Manoribel Hotel
Manori
Talzan
Charkop
Kandivli
MG Road
Marve jetty
Marve Road
Temple
Manori jetty
Marve jn

1 Hillock
2 Gorai dumping ground
3 Bhakti Complex police booth

TO GORAI JETTY

Gorai junction to Gorai jetty, c. 3 km

Stunted mangrove and some salt-flats line this stretch, and the Pacific Golden Plover has often been sighted in vivid breeding plumage in mid-April. With permission, the dense orchard of mango, *chiku* and cashew, that combines with other vegetation to form an evergreen mini-forest, can be explored for a rewarding bird-watch, midway along the trail. Bulbuls, doves, crag martins, swallows, bee-eaters and the occasional Common Babbler add to the bird-list on and around the adjacent rocky hillock, on which a nest of Common Indian Nightjar has been found. Jackal may emerge on this hillock that offers spectacular sights of the sprawling creek and Uttan-Gorai verdure. A Jungle Cat may sneak by or a Bengal Monitor amble across. The road to Gorai jetty, lined by mangroves, Toothbrush Plant and other dense growth, is a haven for White-eared Bulbuls. Swarms of noisy Rosy Starling alight on fruiting Toothbrush Plants in March. The only sighting of Greylag Geese in Mumbai proper was along this stretch. The noisy calls of rails, bitterns and armies of warblers fill the air as waders, crabs, mudskippers and aquatic snakes are seen around the jetty at low tide.

Mudskippers emerge on mudflats at low tide.

TO BHAYANDAR SALT-PANS

Gorai junction to salt-pans on Uttan-Bhayandar Road, 9 km

The trail traverses 2 km of a low ridge, its bulbul-infested greenery derived from private orchards of mango, *chiku*, jackfruit and other tree-growth. Scrub vegetation increases towards Maxwell Hotel. A nearby mango grove harbours typical shade-loving birds such as flycatchers, sunbirds and ioras. The Blue-capped Rock Thrush was sighted in February 2003. A large rain-filled depression to the left of the road is a promising nature site.

The country between Uttan junction and Dongri village is dominated by a low, wooded ridge, lush with paddy fields in the monsoon. In winter, the bird tally can reach a high of 40 species. En route to Dongri is a disused quarry where a lone Eurasian Eagle Owl was sighted in 2002. Towards Bhayandar, dense verdure gives way to open country, salt-

Dense verdure at Dongri Dhakka, with the wide mouth of Bassein Creek in view (above). The rocky, scrub-encrusted hillock between the Gorai junction and the jetty, provides a panoramic view of Manori Creek, dense orchard and extensive scrub and countryside (top).

pans and saline flats. Sparse mangroves brush the southern fringes of Bassein Creek where there is a possibility of sighting small flocks of waders. Ten Lesser Flamingos were seen here on two consecutive days in December 2001.

TO DONGRI DHAKKA   *Uttan junction to Dongri Dhakka (Chowk jetty), 3.5 km*

The Gorai-Bhayandar Road divides at Uttan junction, the west fork leading to Uttan town and Dongri Dhakka, near the mouth of Bassein Creek. En route, a road wends left to the rocky shore past Bhaiti in sight of the small islet of Uttan-Vashi. The Little Tern used to nest on the islet until at least the early 1980s. An almost unbroken string of fishing communities lines the coastal drive to Dongri Dhakka where Bassein Creek's mouth stretches wide amid extensive mangroves. A sandy islet, accessible by boat, could display a congregation of waders, gulls and terns on a good day, while the ruins of Bassein Fort are spotted across the water.

NIRMAL & KELVE

NIRMAL *North of Mumbai; 67 km to Vighaleshwar Lake*
KELVE *North of Mumbai; 110 km to Kelve beach*

LARGE CONGREGATIONS OF WADERS, including godwits, turnstones and oystercatchers, have been intermittently observed on the extensive coastal stretch from Nirmal to Kelve. Well linked by rail and road, the area around is a mix of scrub, cultivation and habitation. Tandulwadi is one of the peaks in the hills ranging west of NH-8, along which are forested pockets, delightful in the monsoon. *See map on page 36.*

EN ROUTE TO ARNALA   *Nalla Sopara junction (NH-8) to Arnala, 26 km*
Suprisingly, a small flock of the disappearing White-rumped Vulture can still be seen in the crowded little town of Santosh Bhavan. Among the numerous avian species on Nirmal's Vighaleshwar Lake are Spot-billed Duck, Pintail, Wigeon, Garganey, Glossy Ibis, Osprey, and even sporadic River Terns. A few Comb Duck, the largest resident waterfowl of peninsular India, are occasionally observed. The birds briefly disappear when the lake is periodically cleared of weeds. The small creek near Nirmal sometimes has a few screaming Caspian Terns, their numbers dropping in the region. Sadly,

Lined with a virtual forest of towering Casuarina trees, the Kelve-Mahim beach is one of the longest and most rewarding of coastal tracts in the region.

several wetland sites, delightfully crammed with herbage and waterfowl, are losing to rising urbanization.

Kalamb beach, reached via a narrow path, is fringed by cultivation. Ruddy Turnstone, Pallas's Gull and Heuglin's Gull can be the birdwatcher's treat. More birds are usually seen to the north on Rajwadi beach, bordered by vibrantly-coloured marigold and sunflower cultivation that is a magnet for butterflies as well. The 12-km stretch from Nirmal to Arnala is a blend of groves and cultivation, but poorly managed tourism has almost reduced Arnala beach to filth.

The uncommon Comb Duck (above right) on Vighaleshwar Lake. A small flock of White-rumped Vultures (top). The imposing Tandulwadi mountain (below) overlooks the winding Vaitarna River.

EN ROUTE TO KELVE BEACH *Varai junction (NH-8) to Kelve beach, 33 km*
A drive left from Varai junction leads to Datiwere and Kelve. Light deciduous forest harbouring Large Cuckoo Shrike and Blue-winged Leafbird along the first 3 km offers some pleasant birdwatching moments. The forest disappears into cultivation and scrub, where Painted Francolin is vocal in the monsoon.

The bridge on Vaitarna River, 11 km from Varai junction, can offer glimpses of such waterside birds as kingfishers, herons, wagtails and, perhaps, Imperial and Short-toed Eagles overhead. Tandulwadi (460 m), its towering, rocky crag a striking feature of the landscape here, can be an excellent monsoon trek via a spur of the hill, shortly past the bridge. The mountain top has dry scrub and cacti around numerous water cisterns, and a panoramic view. The terrain around is encrusted with scrub and sparse mixed-deciduous forest, with ample bamboo, and some fine birding is assured. The long, wide and clean beach of Datiwere, about 25 km from the bridge is fringed by scrub and grass. The highly vocal Grey Francolin, widespread over north and central India, has been heard and spotted here, indicating a possible recent dispersal into north Konkan. The marine life is rich and varied.

En route to Kelve, Makunsar Creek could be a rewarding stop. Soon the creek-side terrain is overrun by verdure, which gives way to lush plantations and dense groves. Lofty Casuarinas (Whistling Pine), evergreens native to the Andaman and Nicobar Islands, line the scenic and long Kelve beach-front, a part of it becoming increasingly crowded with visitors, but a long stretch offers a smattering of waders, gulls and terns. The White-bellied Sea Eagle is intermittently seen and the Peregrine Falcon appears in winter. On the far north is Mahim beach. On the return journey to Mumbai, the tree-dotted scrub habitat before Palghar is good for francolins, quails and other birds of open scrub, especially in the rains. Highly recommended are halts at the enchanting Devkop Lake and the nearby forest towards Sajanpada, on the route from Palghar junction to Manor and NH-8.

Datiwere beach is a haven for waders, gulls, terns and small bands of flamingos during winter.

SEWRI
SE Mumbai; 5 km to Colgate factory

A REMARKABLE SPREAD OF OOZE AND MANGROVE on the west of Thane Creek's wide mouth has of late generated more interest in Mumbai's birds and environment than any other site. The Sewri mudflats seem to willy-nilly accumulate organic richness to draw immense congregations of featherfolk that feast on molluscs, crustaceans, aquatic insects, worms and even smaller life-forms. Somewhat clogged by silt, the bay is ideally calm for waders – from towering flamingos, herons and godwits to smaller sandpipers, dunlins, plovers and minuscule stints. Flamingos, seen from mid-October to May, form an endless arc at low tide, but congregate in dense clusters when the tide turns. The Lesser Flamingo are usually in majority, and together with the Greater Flamingo are estimated to number ten to fifteen thousand. Juveniles and sub-adults are plentiful. Gulls carpet the mudflats in winter, a flush of white and rosy pink set poignantly against a backdrop of blazing furnaces and refineries. This scene could well become Mumbai's major attraction.

Crowds of lanky, colourful flamingos.

THANE CREEK
East of Mumbai, 15 km to Vashi bridge; c. 20 km to Airoli bridge

THANE CREEK EXTENDS for nearly 15 km along the perimeters of Mumbai's eastern suburbs, defined by the Eastern Express Highway to Thane. The creek can be crossed at Vashi bridge as well as Airoli bridge further north, both exceptional viewing sites for birds. Ecologically, the most significant of Mumbai's wetland sites, the total area of the creek, mudflats and mangroves extends over 4000 ha, inclusive of the 700-ha Godrej Pirojshanagar site. According to Vivek Kulkarni of the Godrej Mangrove Project, the area from Kanjurmarg to Airoli bridge has been proposed as a nature park, and much of Thane Creek and its environs could be declared a wetland site of international importance.

Avian species sighted around Thane Creek number nearly 200, including scrub and grass birds, with the majority on the creek's western bank where there is less industry and housing development. The creek also sustains the longest surviving stretch of mangrove in the region. Several species occur here, together with associate plants such as Sea Holly, Indian Saltwort and Mangrove Beanstalk, which blooms white early in the year, attracting ants and bees. A densely growing, succulent herb, Shore Purselane's pink flowers bloom

Extensive, healthy mangroves and vast mudflats edge the Thane Creek, which is visited by huge congregations of birds and other wildlife.

on maroon-red branches also at this time. The
sweet red berries of Toothbrush Plant appear in
March-April, drawing in birds, particularly swarms
of Rosy Starlings.

Creek and mangrove together support a range
of life-forms – microscopic plants, zooplanktons,
crustaceans, molluscs and a variety of fish and
reptiles such as Glossy Marsh Snake and Dog-faced
Water Snake. Vivek Kulkarni says; "Mangroves
play a crucial role in maintaining Mumbai harbour
and navigation routes in optimum condition."
They control sedimentation, which is reaching
alarming proportions in Mumbai Port, despite
quarterly dredging.

*The mangroves of Thane Creek
harbour a sizeable population
of the largely elusive
Clamorous Reed Warbler.*

VASHI BRIDGE

The reeking dumping grounds of Deonar en route from Sion, lure numerous
raptors, including the large, dark-plumaged *Aquila* eagles that are both hunters
and scavengers.

Intermittent
congregations of waders
line the highway on
sheltered mudflats during
high tide, especially along
Mankhurd.

Permission can be
sought from the police
post at the western end to
walk along the old
disused bridge, adjacent to
the busy modern one, to
achieve a bird's-eye view
of the creek's environs
and the birds themselves.
North of the bridge, a
maze of transmission
towers is crammed with

*The road to Bhandup's BMC
Lagoon runs along the side
channels of the creek (right).
Wintering gulls on Thane
Creek (above right).*

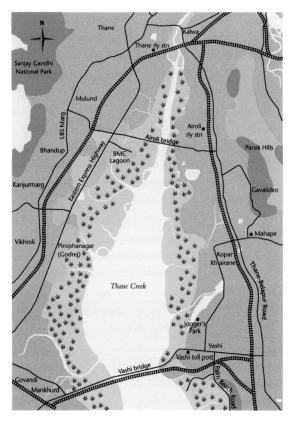

roosting raptors, mostly the common Black Kite, with perhaps a majestic White-bellied Sea Eagle. Osprey and falcons have been sighted, apart from *Aquila* eagles, usually seen post-monsoon.

Past the east end of the bridge, good birdwatching can be had at the disused hovercraft landing jetty and Jogger's Park in Navi Mumbai. Scrub and mangrove offer glimpses of Clamorous Reed Warbler, White-eared Bulbul and Bluethroat, as warblers flit about and a multitude of crabs, mudskippers and aquatic snakes lurk in the glistening ooze.

AIROLI BRIDGE *Permission required from security cabin at west end of bridge*
The mangroves, scrub and pools of water on either side of Bhandup's BMC Lagoon (Mumbai Sewage Disposal Project) – off the Eastern Express Highway, and shortly before the turning for the Airoli bridge – host reptiles and insects as well as birds such as White-eared Bulbul, Clamorous Reed Warbler, White-throated Fantail, Bluethroat, Grey Heron, Little Heron and Yellow Bittern. The White Stork, a winter migrant from eastern Europe, was regularly reported through the 1970s up until the mid-1980s.

The salt-pans, marshes, mangroves and mudflats on either side of the creek at Airoli bridge display larger congregations of migrant waders, terns and gulls between October and April. Low tide brings a variety of waders, from tiny stints to towering godwits, the bridge providing a panoramic view of both creek and birds from above. Flamingos, perhaps spilling over from neighbouring Sewri, are sometimes sighted on the southern banks of the creek.

Uran

SE of Mumbai; c. 40 km to JNPT police station

VERY ACCESSIBLE BUT SURROUNDED BY activity related to the Jawaharlal Nehru Port Trust (JNPT), Uran is an increasingly popular birding haven. Its mix of habitats – reed-encrusted depressions, open marshes, mangrove-edged creek, grass, scrub, seasonal cultivation, salt-flats and barren tracts, as well as nutrient-rich sea water and rain-fed freshwater – has led to a bird list of nearly 160 species. An immense number of waders, including small parties of flamingos, spoonbills, storks and ibises, as well as open-land birds and a sprinkling of raptors can be easily observed, often even from the comfort of the car. The first confirmed breeding of Black-breasted Weaver in the Mumbai region was reported in Uran during the monsoon of 2002.

While the marshes are chock-full with endlessly dribbling waders, there are ample sightings of falcons, kites, kingfishers, bee-eaters, shrikes, rollers, chats and doves on roadside electric poles and overhead cables. From October to early April, the birdwatcher can easily sight up to 90 species within four hours, the number dropping to about 40 for the rest of the year.

Of mammals, the most widespread appears to be the Jackal. Sometimes a family appears on the edge of a reed-encrusted marsh, causing a flutter amongst the waders and waterfowl. The occasional mongoose pair can result

The extensive marshes of Uran draw great congregations of wintering waders.

The largest number of Grey Herons in the Mumbai region are sighted in Uran. These lanky birds rarely mix actively with other waders.

in a similar uproar. The odd Jungle Cat is present and local inhabitants report the presence of a Striped Hyena, although it has been almost a decade since one was seen.

EN ROUTE TO CBD-BELAPUR JUNCTION
Vashi toll post to CBD-Belapur junction, 10 km

The large Karave pond, 5.5 km from Vashi toll post, is the first major halt on the drive to Uran. With a regulated inflow of sea water, it is excellent for viewing the herons, gulls and terns that are attracted to the fisherfolk's activities. The Caspian Tern, India's largest tern, is an almost guaranteed sight as it screams and plunges for fish and crabs. The shallow marsh behind TS Chanakya, a naval training school, just over a kilometre from the pond, is usually crammed with waders, numerous sandpipers and plovers between October and April. A few waterfowl, including Garganey and Pintail, and small flocks of flamingos, ibises and spoonbills are occasionally seen, while the open scrub around is the haunt of stonechats, shrikes, larks, pipits and doves. The tree-lined stretch west of the marsh has a few small heronries. The reed-beds, pond and creek inlets just past the Sea Woods Complex prove that birds rule the roost so far, despite unremitting developmental pressures.

Vashi toll post
Palm Beach Road
Karave pond
CBD-Belapur jn
Trombay
Thane Creek
1
2
Panvel Creek
Uran Road
Elephanta Is
Nhava
Vahal
3
to Panvel →
Kopar
Butcher Is
JNPT
Jasai
Sheva Creek
Mora
Panje
5
4
Uran Road
Dongri
Funde
7
6
Panvel JNPT Road
Kegaon
8
Uran
Dronagiri
Karanjia

1 TS Chanakya marsh
2 Sea Woods Complex
3 Gawanpada
4 JNPT railway crossing
5 JNPT marsh
6 JNPT police station
7 Uran marsh
8 Hotel Uran Plaza

EN ROUTE TO JASAI

CBD-Belapur junction to Jasai, 9.5 km

Some marshy areas occur between Panvel Creek bridge and Gawanpada, and should be investigated for waders such as the gregarious Ruff and the Common Redshank. The rarely seen Red Knot and Broad-billed Sandpiper have been sighted here. A few Baobab trees stand to the left of Uran Road and around Vahal village, 4.5 km from the

The Black-breasted Weaver was first sighted in Uran during 2002 monsoon.

junction, is some light deciduous forest and a dense stretch of bamboos. In the monsoon, babblers, cuckoos and Jungle Bush Quails announce their presence. The road divides at Gawanpada, the narrower bifurcation leading right through scrub, cultivation and an expansive creek-side sprawl to Nhava, while the other leads left to Jasai, through a disturbed stretch along the Panvel-Uran Road. However, occasional raptors perched on transmission towers, including Laggar Falcon and Short-toed Eagle may keep the birdwatcher's interest alive. At Jasai, the terrain opens on to grass- and reed-encrusted marsh, and the finest bird halts lie ahead.

On the route to Nhava, the first 3 km to Kopar village run through lush green cultivation, perfect terrain for Rat Snakes and Bengal Monitors. Low mangroves later dominate the landscape. Roadside grass growth and a riot of herbage in the monsoon includes Glory Lily, Common Balsam, Common Borage and Silver Spiked Cockscomb. The White-eared Bulbul is commonly encountered while Bluethroat, Stonechat, Long-tailed Shrike and warblers enhance the bird count in winter. Besides the ubiquitous Black Kite, raptors include winter migrants such as Marsh Harrier, Hen Harrier, Black-shouldered Kite, Laggar Falcon, Osprey and Brahminy Kite. This is also where a solitary Black Bittern was sighted in August 2003. Inlets and mud-flats sustain a few waders, and small heronries around Nhava host nesting cormorants and herons. The Jackal is seen on the road at dusk or night, while the Jungle Cat remains elusive.

Fishermen and birds at dawn, on the sprawling Karave pond along the Palm Beach Road.

EN ROUTE TO URAN *Jasai to JNPT police station, 5.5 km*

The inundated marshes, salt-flats and open lands on either side of Uran Road, soon after Jasai, swarm with waders, including flocks of Little and Temminck's Stints, the smallest of India's migratory waders. The 4 km stretch from Jasai to the Karal flyover, a spectacular mix of wetland habitats, is crammed with bird species. There is a variety of aquatic types, from herons, waterfowl and waders, to ibises, spoonbills and jacanas.

This is the finest stretch to view Glossy Ibis, a gregarious winter visitor that can be seen feeding in shallow waters. In the monsoon of 2002, the breeding Black-breasted Weaver, sporting a vivid yellow crown, was sighted here, perhaps the first confirmed report of the bird in the western peninsula. The adjacent drier tracts teem with larks. Congregations of Short-toed Lark and Black-headed Bunting arrive in winter.

Past the flyover, a sharp turn to the left, off Uran Road, leads to JNPT police station, and the marsh opposite. The endless bird-list includes avocets, godwits, flamingos, spoonbills and ibises. Ruddy Shelduck and Spotted Redshank can also be seen. A small flock of Jungle Myna has been sighted and the bird could be more prevalent than assumed. On occasion, jackals lurking in the reeds charge at the waterfowl, causing a flurry of activity.

Huge congregations of waders on a winter morning near Funde.

TRAIL BEHIND MARSH

JNPT marsh to Funde, 6.5 km ▶▶

An unpaved dirt-track, only seasonally motorable, is a highly recommended bird walk through an open wetland habitat of marsh, mud-flat, salt-pan, scrub and mangrove. Small trees such as *Parkinsonia aculeata*, Australian Acacia and Su-babul line the intersecting paths and serve as ideal perches for birds. During October to early April, three to four hours could result in a tally of 60-70 bird species. Mangrove-lined salt-pans occur towards the villages of Dongri and Panje, in the latter half of the trail. The main trail heads towards the motorable road leading directly from JNPT police station to Funde village, which is a less arduous journey than the 6.5 km detour. Some of Uran's finest birding sites lie towards its main road, a string of roadside marshes providing some close sightings of waders, including large flocks of godwits, Black-winged Stilt and Pied Avocet. At times as many as 150 avocets have been sighted from as close as 15 m, their long curved beaks gracefully sweeping the waters for food.

TO PANJE   *Funde to Panje, 3 km*

The marshes, inundated salt- and mud-flats near Funde are often choked with waders, including large flocks of stints, avocets, godwits and other sandpipers. There are fairly regular sightings of the wintering Slender-billed Gull, a species easily confused with the more familiar Black-headed Gull. The route, passing by Dongri village, offers a sprinkling of creek-side, marsh and scrub birds. The hillock of Panje overlooks Sheva Creek as well as Elephanta and Butcher islands. Spots worth investigating include the area around Kegaon towards the west, where Hotel Uran Plaza, spread over 3.5 ha on a west-facing beach, provides a comfortable overnight halt. At Karanjia, a ferry ride across Dharamtar Creek towards Rewas can be a memorable nature-watch.

The Greater Painted Snipe is a secretive, polyandrous bird, the female more showy and demonstrative.

MANDWA, ALIBAUG & MURUD–JANJIRA

MANDWA *South of Mumbai; c. 118 km to Mandwa jetty*
MURUD *South of Mumbai; c. 140 km to Murud*

ACROSS THE SEA FROM MUMBAI HARBOUR, the narrow expanse of coastal land, from Rewas and Mandwa to Alibaug, is a pleasantly secluded stretch of orchards, private estates and quaint villages with some fine beaches and sylvan countryside. It is sprinkled with ancient Banyan, towering Casuarina and Black Plum (*jamun*), the calm interrupted by sharp cries of the glorious male Paradise Flycatcher, the delightful rambling notes of the White-browed Fantail, and the victorious Shikra as it ambushes its prey. The ferry ride from Mumbai takes under an hour to Mandwa, but the drive is unusually scenic.

South of Alibaug is verdant seaside country with orchards, cultivation, sleepy habitations, sandy beaches, creeks and inlets. Low, forested hills rise to the east. In a spectacular mix of nature and history, the area offers the sightseer ancient temples, forts, palaces, and the ruins of Portuguese churches.

EN ROUTE TO MANDWA *Vadhkal junction (NH-17) to Mandwa, 32 km*
This long stretch through open land, grass and monsoon cultivation, lined with some Khejri (*Prosopis*), Babul, Manila Tamarind, Indian Jujube (*ber*) and

The White-bellied Sea Eagle, among the most impressive of the region's raptors, can be sighted along coastal stretches, and perhaps still breeds in the Alibaug-Murud stretch.

Australian Acacia, is a fine habitat for larks, pipits, wagtails, stonechats, lapwings, shrikes, doves, harriers, Indian Roller and Black-shouldered Kite. At low tide, terns, gulls, and a few waders dash about on Dharamtar Creek, 3 km from Vadhkal junction. The open grass on either side of the creek can be explored for elusive rails, crakes and quails while warblers flit actively during the monsoon.

After Poynad, 6.5 km from Vadhkal junction, grass and scrub give way to taller roadside trees, flanked by private farms and orchards. A small pond, a few kilometres further, usually has a pair or two of Little Grebe, the smallest of India's waterfowl. Tall deciduous forest covers a ridge

The famed Baya Weaver is a frequent sight in open country at the onset of the monsoon.

that extends from close to the coast and harbours isolated populations of several woodland birds. At Karlekhind, a road to the right (north) offers a pleasant drive to Saral, from where the road again branches right towards Rewas jetty, overlooking Dharamtar Creek. For over a kilometre from Saral, the sandy coast on the left teems with avian congregations that could include the uncommon Great-crested Tern and Caspian Tern. On the right is an extensive salt-flat, and in the dry season, between October and April, there is a possibility of sighting the Stone Curlew, besides Desert Wheatear, stonechats, lapwings, and maybe pratincoles. The extensive mangroves along the road are mostly stunted.

From Saral, the road west leads to Mandwa, and the occasional kingfisher and heron or some terns can be expected along the initial inundated stretch. Mandwa is largely open scrub and private orchards. The Eurasian Eagle Owl once frequented the disused quarries, and may still occur. Mandwa's stretch of beach is relatively clean but the number and variety of waders, including Ruddy Turnstone and Oystercatcher, is very small. Kankeshwar Temple nestles close-by in a hilltop forest, reached via a steep ascent, but worth a nature-lover's ramble.

Greatly altered by cultivation, orchards and private estates, the Alibaug-Mandwa stretch still retains a distinctly rural atmosphere.

The end of monsoon brings swarms of dragonflies (top) to the marshes, and colourful bee-eaters (above) feast on this bounty.

EN ROUTE TO KIHIM

Rewas junction to Kihim, 9 km

Off the Alibaug-Mandwa Road, about 3 km from Rewas junction, is Dhokavde pond, encircled by large trees. It draws a few waterfowl, jacanas, herons and kingfishers. Pleasantly quiet lanes resound with quail and cuckoo calls in the monsoon, and also harbour other scrub birds. The approach to Kihim is via Chondhi on the Alibaug-Mandwa Road. The main beach of Kihim is somewhat crowded, but its secluded northern stretch is lined with lofty trees and old cottages, including those of the great ornithologists, the late Dr Salim Ali and Humayun Abdulali. Flycatchers, sunbirds and woodpeckers are only a few of the many birds here. Until recently, a towering Casuarina tree was the nesting site of a White-bellied Sea Eagle.

EN ROUTE TO KORLAI

BEACH *Alibaug to Korlai beach, 21 km*

South of Alibaug, along the road to Murud, is Sakhar Khadi, a stretch of creek flanked by stunted mangroves that may surprise the birdwatcher with a Reef Egret or Black-capped Kingfisher, while Desert Wheatear and Hoopoe probe the banks. A diversion to the right then leads to Akshi beach, a long clean water-front boasting a dense Casuarina plantation. It teems with marine life and the many bird species seen include Sandwich Tern, Great-crested Tern, Slender-billed Gull, Oystercatcher, Ruddy Turnstone and White-bellied Sea Eagle.

Lush verdure, coconut and betel-nut plantations, and a string of traditional cottages dominate the first 15 km of the Alibaug-Murud Road, and host orioles, flycatchers, sunbirds, flowerpeckers and bulbuls. At Revdanda stand the ruins of a 350-year-old Jesuit monastery, overgrown with foliage and some Banyan trees. Not far is the bridge over Revdanda Creek, worth a quick look for herons, gulls and terns. To the west is a small hill, topped by the ancient Korlai Fort, overgrown, and with numerous lizards and snakes.

Dhokavde pond is one of the few waterbodies in the area that still retain some herbage.

Korlai offers a splendidly clean and golden beach-front. Below the fort in the north and towards the lighthouse, a leisurely walk may yield harriers, a few waders, stonechats, bee-eaters, hoopoe and shrikes. The few large trees here are the evergreen Portia, distinguished by large heart-shaped leaves and yellow flowers that appear between December and May. It is just over a 100 m climb to the fort, from where the Kundalika River can be witnessed as it empties into Revdanda Creek to the background music of screaming gulls and terns. A Common Kestrel dashes past, a lone Pallid Harrier circles close-by, and Dusky Crag Martins and Red-rumped Swallows go about their business. The reptile clan includes Saw-scaled Viper and several rock geckos.

A mix of sandy and rocky shore, the Kashid beach is located on the picturesque Alibaug-Murud stretch.

The brick-red winged fruits of Flowering Murdals.

EN ROUTE TO AGARDANDA
Korlai to Agardanda, c. 36 km

Just a ten-minute drive from Revdanda bridge, on the Alibaug-Murud Road, there is a stunning view of the long, ribbon-like beach of Kashid, its white sands fringed with dense Casuarina that blends into the forested hills edging Phansad Wildlife Sanctuary. The drive itself is among the most scenic in the region, with forest and exquisite sea-front on either side, but hosting very few waders, gulls and terns. Of pelagic birds, rarities such as Masked Booby and Lesser Frigatebird have been sighted in the monsoon, and there is a recent report of a Red-billed Tropicbird. The dramatic White-bellied Sea Eagle is more regularly encountered here than elsewhere on the region's coast.

Between Kashid and Nandgaon, the sandy and rocky coastline is fringed with scrub, cultivation, and a string of resorts. From Nandgaon, a route leads to the main gate of Phansad Wildlife Sanctuary, 4.5 km away, while the coastal road continues towards Murud, Janjira and Agardanda. The long, scenic, winding drive suddenly reveals the creamy expanse of Murud beach on the gleaming Arabian Sea. Undulating, wooded terrain lies to the east.

The 5 km drive to Janjira skirts a small creek, and a short ascent later offers a view of the creek and some herons and kingfishers, as Indian Grey Hornbills feast on the berries of roadside Banyan trees. The seaward hill slopes are dotted with Purging Nut and Common Chaste Tree. The imposing Janjira Fort forms the backdrop to hoopoes and Green Bee-eaters. Nearby Khokri is worth a visit for the region's largest collection of Baobab trees — eleven enormous specimens. The vicinity's ruins harbour lizards and provide roosts, and occasionally nesting sites, to a few swifts, swallows and martins. The plantations and groves around Agardanda, just a short drive away, are delight to explore. From a small jetty, a ferry plies to Dighi, as gulls and terns scream past and flashy parakeets feed on *Ficus* berries.

The gigantic Baobab trees.

URBAN SITES

ESSELWORLD
NW Mumbai; 31 km to Borivli jetty, 50 km by road via Dahisar Check Naka

SITUATED ON A LOW GRADIENT on the western margin of Manori Creek, Esselworld is India's largest amusement park. Along with the adjoining Water Kingdom, a water theme park, it occupies an area of 26 ha. A strip of dense mangrove near the Esselworld jetty overlooks Talzan hill on the east, while stunted mangroves fringe the west and south margins. Some areas have salt-flats, but much of the park is a veritable forest that includes hoary *Ficus* trees. Since its inception in the 1980s, when there was generally an inadequate and poor awareness of ecological issues, the management has been increasingly conscious of preserving the environment. A well-stocked in-house nursery rears several thousand saplings of endemic and exotic species, including a large number of mangroves.

Over a hundred thousand shrubs and trees have been planted here, transforming Esselworld into a haven for parkland and scrubland birds such as drongos, fantails, bulbuls, sunbirds, ioras, several warblers, doves, Crow Pheasant and the occasional Shikra. Among the plants are about 80 species of trees, over 100 of herbs and shrubs, and numerous creepers, climbers and palms. The lush foliage lends a very tropical ambience and well-laid roads

The tree-lined paths at Esselworld and Water Kingdom come as a wonderful surprise, clearly indicative of a rising concern for environment among corporates today.

combine for fairly rewarding rambles to observe birds, insects, and above all, a wealth of plants. The numerous reptiles include Bengal Monitor, and trained staff can handle and rescue snakes rather than kill them on sight. Jackals and the occasional Jungle Cat continue to lurk about and as many as 31 varieties of butterflies have been observed so far. With thousands of daily visitors, the twin parks offer a classic opportunity for combining fun with education. The park observes many environment-friendly practices, including waste-water and sewage treatment, and vermiculture, and visits to these critical facilities are encouraged. Esselworld's parent company, Pan India Paryatan Limited, hopes to develop some of the surrounding property into a unique mangrove park for exploring the secrets of this irreplaceable ecosystem. *See map on page 96.*

Top to bottom: *A Magpie Robin momentarily settles on a visitor's handbag. A beautifully patterned dragonfly basks in the warm sun. The evergreen Devil's Tree is widely planted at the site.*

IIT CAMPUS & POWAI LAKE

North Mumbai; 18 km to main gate. Permission required for day visits from security booth at gate

SITUATED ON THE CROWDED ADI SHANKARACHARYA ROAD, the main entrance to IIT (Indian Institute of Technology) provides access to a campus that spreads over 200 ha on the eastern margin of Powai Lake.

The 160-ha lake was created in 1891 and is now almost locked in by large residential and commercial complexes. Effluents have dangerously damaged its ecosystem. Lately, the prolific Water Hyacinth has occupied some of the lake's surface, while the shore supports Marsh Glory, Castor Oil Plant, Marsh Barbel and several other herbs and shrubs. The lake is almost contiguous with the Sanjay Gandhi National Park in the north. A viewing platform on AS Road reveals a winter high of 30 bird species, perhaps including a few Glossy Ibis and Asian Openbill. More frequently seen are egrets, herons, cormorants, Purple Swamphen and Lesser Whistling Duck. Snipes, waterhen, moorhen and perhaps a few more rails and crakes lurk in the marsh. Expect to see Marsh Harrier and several terns in winter. Mugger (Marsh Crocodile) have often been sighted, and one even appeared on the busy AS Road. The tall dense verdure of the 11-ha Ambedkar Garden on Powai's western fringe, hosts a few edge-of-forest birds, making for a delightful morning stroll.

Its water may not be potable, but the open, grassy margins of Powai Lake continue to draw a flurry of featherfolk.

Two lush parks, Nirvana Park and Forest Garden, south of the lake and in the prestigious Hiranandani residential complex, offer a choice of shrubs and trees that, over time, have attracted numerous insects and reptiles. Bulbuls, golden orioles, paradise flycatchers, greater coucals, coppersmith barbets, tailorbirds, sunbirds, and even an occasional Shikra could be chanced upon. The Ashy Drongo has been seen twice in winter.

A Lemon Pansy butterfly basks on an October morning.

EAST TRAIL   *Main gate to Market gate, 3.5 km. Permission required*
From the main road leading from the gate, by-roads run left to unobstructed views of Powai Lake. A sprinkling of exotic flora and numerous endemic species of trees, including Variegated Bauhinia, Indian Coral, Soccerball Tree, Karanj, Karaya and Flame of the Forest result in a forest-like terrain that sustains up to 30-40 species of birds. Leopard is often sighted, infiltrating the campus from the neighbouring forest of the national park. The trail continues towards the electronics research institute, Sameer, where a wooded incline presents the national park hills to the north. Skirting the Kendriya Vidyalaya, this leisurely but circuitous walk to the market gate takes under two hours.

LAKESIDE TRAIL   *Hostel 8 to boathouse, 1.2 km*
Just past Hostel 8 on the main campus road, a narrow trail leads to an old, dilapidated boathouse amid lofty, somewhat overgrown trees. A surprisingly large number of Black Kites have made their roost on the lakeside.

Scores of aquatic birds, the occasional Mugger, Bengal Monitor, and perhaps even a Rock Python or Common Mongoose, can be seen against either the lush water-front or the Hiranandani Gardens complex to the south.

The main path from Hostel 8 leads south towards the lakeside guest-houses and Devi Mandir on the lake's eastern edge.

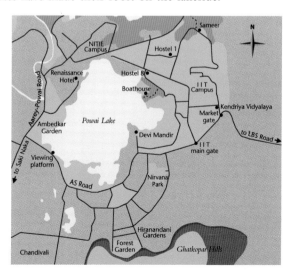

PIROJSHANAGAR (GODREJ ESTATES)

NE Mumbai; 12 km to main gate. Permission required

IN 1943, THE GODREJ FAMILY purchased property at Vikhroli, then a desolate eastern suburb west of Thane Creek. Thousands of trees were planted and parks created before the 1200-ha industrial township of Pirojshanagar was established. Nearly 700 ha of this is covered with dense mangrove.

The finest of Mumbai's mangroves extend for over 5 km along the creek, home to over 20 species of fish, at least 13 of crabs and 7 of prawns, besides other life-forms. The scrub and open grass that span the stretch to the Eastern Express Highway form a significant lark, warbler and munia habitat, with up to four species of each breeding here in the monsoon, when wild grasses, herbs and shrubs proliferate. Winter brings an invasion of migrant birds.

The restricted area sprawling between the highway and Lal Bahadur Shastri Marg is heavily

The wintering Black-shouldered Kite scans the grounds for grasshoppers and lizards (left). Pirojshanagar is a glowing example of how corporate interests and environmental concerns can dovetail, resulting in a thriving ecosystem within city limits (top).

dotted by lofty trees and expansive lawns, the
vegetation a mix of ornamental flora and endemic
species, which include uncommon plants such as
Cannonball Tree, Kadamb, Tolu Balsam Tree and
Potato Tree. With Thane Creek so near, several
heronries are found within this industrial part of
Pirojshanagar. They spread along Peltophorum
Avenue, around Plants 11 and 12, and along the
stretch from Plants 13 to 18. The monotonous,
recurring calls of Coppersmith Barbet, the fluty
notes of golden orioles, cheery bulbuls, and lively
tailorbirds are audible over the clang of industry
and the roar of trains along the busy Central

Railway route that
passes through the
estate.

The area west of
LBS Marg is fringed by
the hills of Ghatkopar to
the south and Powai
Lake to the north. The
Leopard was sighted
recently, evidently a
stray from Sanjay
Gandhi National Park,
just over 6 km to the
northwest. Particular
care has been taken to
nurture the ample scrub
and light forest of this
largely inhabited stretch.
Pirojshanagar remains
the foremost model of
corporate interests
dovetailing
environmental concerns.
See map on page 104.

*A glorious burst of Indian
Laburnum in summer* (right).
*The grasshopper is a very
important part of the food
chain* (top).

MAHARASHTRA NATURE PARK

West Mumbai; 1.5 km to main gate. Permission required

LOCATED AT THE EDGE OF MAHIM CREEK, the 14-ha Maharashtra Nature Park is a verdant realm of forest in a vastly polluted and populated stretch. The sluggish Mithi River skirts the park's northern boundary, emptying its effluence into Mahim Creek. Asia's largest slum, Dharavi, edges the park to the south. In its pristine form, this area would have been a mangrove-encrusted paradise, but long use as one of Mumbai's garbage dumps had choked both the creek and its vegetation.

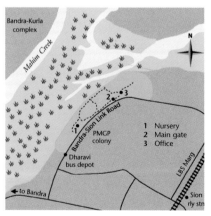

In 1982-83, concerned individuals, the World Wide Fund for India, and government bodies such as Mumbai's municipal corporation and its Metropolitan Region Development Authority, combined their efforts to salvage this site, strongly supported by SP Godrej, the late chairman of the Godrej group of

The Red-vented Bulbul has readily adapted to an urban environment, and can be seen in Mumbai city's parks and gardens.

companies. Renowned ornithologist, Salim Ali, planted the inaugural tree in 1983 and soon tons of garbage was replaced by soil, first by enthusiastic volunteers and then by a team of workers. In the next three years, several thousand saplings were planted, including five more by Salim Ali in 1987. The park was opened to the public on Earth Day, 22 April 1994.

Today, it has matured into a reasonably dense forest of over 14,000 trees. The 320 species of flora are divided into a Tree Section, a Medicinal Plants Section, which offers saplings and seeds for sale, and the serene Nakshatra Van, a lush green circular garden. Myriad shrubs have come as a bonanza for insects in this part of the city.

With nearly 80 species of birds, 40 of butterflies, and a wealth of other insects, reptiles and amphibians, the park attracts over 50,000 annual visitors. Bird calls and screams of squirrels blur memories of the slums and traffic outside the gate. Mahim Creek, visible from the northern parts of the park, attracts stately Grey Herons, stilts, terns and a few scattered waders that seem unconcerned by the floating filth as they go about their chores against a gleaming backdrop of the Bandra-Kurla complex. The Yellow-footed Green Pigeon, Maharashtra's state bird, was sighted here not long ago.

This nature park is the epitome of human endeavour. It demonstrates how well nature responds to the merest touch of a helping human hand. Mumbai could do with a few more of such areas.

The great variety of planted trees (top) *in the park include several Pipal and Banyan, their figs attracting insects and birds such as the occasional Paradise Flycatcher* (right).

Juhu Aerodrome & Bhavan's College Campus

JUHU AERODROME *North Mumbai; 10 km to gate on SV Road*
BHAVAN'S COLLEGE CAMPUS *North Mumbai; 14 km to Munshi gate*

RESTRICTED TO THE PUBLIC, Juhu Aerodrome, spanning 150 ha of open grass between SV Road and Juhu-Tara Road in Vile Parle, is a refuge for over 50 species of birds and a score of butterflies. It also offers sightings of Common Mongoose, Common Rat Snake and Bengal Monitor. Numerous reptiles such as the odd Spectacled Cobra still lurk amid the grass. Depressions dotting the site usually retain some rain water, even in summer, attracting a range of avifauna, from an almost even mix of grass and scrub species to several waterside birds, some of which breed here. A few kilometres from the aerodrome lie the Airport Authority of India (AAI) grounds, almost 20 ha of marshy grassland, and a birdwatcher's delight. Situated east of Andheri Link Road, it is adjacent to the Bhavan's College where tall trees and a small freshwater pond push the area's bird tally to nearly 70 species. There are a fair number of herons, egrets, cormorants, warblers and even a couple of waterhen through the year, while winter visitors include wagtails, Spotted and Green Sandpipers, Common Stonechat and the occasional Marsh Harrier. To the east stands Gilbert Hill, now shorn of its original foliage that once harboured Jackal. Munshi gate of Bhavan's College offers the best route to these sites.

The small, sheltered pond on Bhavan's College campus is a haven for birds.

VEERMATA JIJABAI BHONSLE UDYAN (BYCULLA ZOO)
Central Mumbai; 9 km to gate

THE VEERMATA JIJABAI BHONSLE UDYAN, formerly Victoria Garden, or simply Byculla Zoo to Mumbai residents, attracts throngs of visitors, who come not only to view animals and birds in cramped cages, but also to explore the tranquil greenery that spreads over around 20 ha. A walk along the network of trails would take not more than an hour, and is a plant-lover's delight. Nearly 3000 trees crowd the area and include more than 175 species, a mix of indigenous and exotic, among which are some of south Mumbai's oldest Baobabs, the ubiquitous Flamboyant (Gulmohar), and the Copper Pod. In the garden's list of rarities are at least three specimens of the small evergreen Flame Amherstia, its drooping scarlet and golden-orange flowers blooming between February and April, Krishna's Buttercup, Calabash Tree, American Sumach, Stinkwood Tree, Australian Chestnut, Fern Tree, Rudraksh, *Kleinhovia* and Talipot Palm. This is one of the few remaining sites in Mumbai where noisy colonies of the Flying Fox are still found, while numerous trees of the fig family attract the much smaller Short-nosed Fruit Bat. Apart from the zoo's collection of birds, its lofty trees and verdure are home to wild-roaming Golden Oriole, Red-vented Bulbul, White-throated Fantail, Magpie Robin, Night Heron as well as the occasional Greater Coucal and Paradise Flycatcher.

The Jijabai Bhonsle Udyan has an abundance of trees that sustain a wealth of birds and insects.

MAHALAXMI RACECOURSE & WILLINGDON SPORTS CLUB
South Mumbai; 14 km to racecourse parking area

DESPITE REAL ESTATE PRICES that compete with the highest in the world, there are a fair number of maidans and clubs in south Mumbai. The sprawling Mahalaxmi Racecourse, managed by the Royal Western Indian Turf Club, stretches between Lala Lajpatrai Marg and Dr E Moses Road, with its main gate off K Khadye Marg. Races are held between November and early April, when a reasonable number of wintering birds such as bee-eaters, wagtails, Long-tailed Shrikes, the occasional Stonechat and Marsh Harrier also converge on this open land. There has even been a solitary sighting of the Eurasian Wryneck. Towards the end of the monsoon and a couple of months thereafter, the site is encrusted with dense grass and herbage. The tree-lined stretch along the southern and eastern margins attracts a few arboreal birds, including Golden Oriole. Across the road spreads the Willingdon Sports Club, open only to members, but one can go as a guest. Almost 30 ha in extent, the grounds support almost 2500 trees, including several endemic species, and never disappoint a birdwatcher. They also host some very hardy insects during the latter half of the monsoon. At least 15 varieties of butterflies have been observed here, besides four of grasshoppers and two of praying mantis.

A profusion of grasshoppers and other insects in the grassy open land of the racecourse attracts myriad birds, including a few raptors.

MALABAR HILL
South Mumbai; 16 km to Hanging Gardens

TODAY, MALABAR HILL BOASTS some of the country's most expensive real estate. Amazingly, 19th-century descriptions stress its densely foliated·terrain, teeming with venomous snakes, jackals and hyenas. Tigers were occasionally sighted here in the late 1700s! Rising urbanization saw the heavy verdure disappear, leaving only small pockets around the Towers of Silence, a restricted area of the Parsi community, and Raj Bhavan, the official residence of the governor of Maharashtra, off Walkeshwar Road. Their ample flora invites Flying Fox, Short-nosed Fruit Bat, Striped Palm Squirrel and several rodents, as well as numerous birds and butterflies. The Raj Bhavan estate displays Teak, · Charcoal Tree, Belleric Myrobalan, Ghost Tree and Red Silk Cotton, remnants of some of the region's primary flora. Over a hundred plant species, at least 40 avian and 34 butterfly species have been identified. The football-sized globular nests of Crematogaster tree-ants have been seen here, as well as a Red-breasted Parakeet pair, probably broken free from captivity. Pherozshah Mehta Garden, originally Hanging Gardens, occupies a part of the ridge, and was laid in the 1880s over a reservoir. The forested slopes of the Towers of Silence adjoin the garden to the east and northeast. The Kamla Nehru Park, across the road, offers fine views of Marine Drive and the city's skyline.

Malabar Hill is possibly the only area in south Mumbai where a bit of original flora still exists.

Sagar Upwan & Colaba Woods

South Mumbai; 20 km to Sagar Upwan

SAGAR UPWAN, the *c.* 5-ha Mumbai Port Trust Garden, behind the Sassoon Dock area of Colaba, is divided into sections specializing in flowering trees, bamboos, exotic species and medicinal plants. There is even an 'astral garden' and a small glasshouse. An in-house sewage treatment plant meets the garden's water requirement. Flame of the Forest, Sissoo, Indian Kino, Bonfire Tree, Indian Cork Tree, Ironwood Tree, and White Silk Cotton or Kapok flourish on this bit of reclaimed land. The Yellow Silk Cotton flowers vividly against azure summer skies, and a row of densely-foliaged Barringtonia trees lines the southern corner. Wildlife has been quick to invade. A list comprising almost 40 bird species includes sunbirds, bulbuls, orioles, tailorbirds and magpie-robins. Aquatic species are attracted to the adjacent water-front. Barn Owls, the occasional Spotted Owlet, and numerous bats become active as dusk falls. Colaba Woods is nearby, close to the World Trade Centre in Cuffe Parade. The site was a dumping ground before the Tata Electric Company created this 3-ha park in the early 1980s. Within the 'forest' of over 2000 trees, Indian Laburnum blooms yellow in the heat of April and May, while Golden Oriole, Purple-rumped Sunbird and Magpie Robin burst into uninhibited melody, and a piercing scream draws attention to a winsome male Paradise Flycatcher.

The brilliant blooms of the Yellow Silk Cotton in early summer.

APPENDIX

CONTACTS

SPECIES LISTING

CONTACTS

Permissions, when required, should be sought from the Forest Office unless otherwise mentioned. Many trails require no permission, but it is advisable to inform the local forest office or staff, wherever present.

CEC (BNHS) Near Film City, Off Western Express Highway, Goregaon (W), Mumbai. Tel 28421174, 28402946. For group visits, advance booking/intimation advised

KARNALA, PHANSAD & TANSA SANCTUARIES Deputy Conservator of Forests (Wildlife) Thane, LBS Road, Naupada, Near Highway Naka, Thane 400 602. Tel 25402522

MAHARASHTRA NATURE PARK Tel 24077641, 24079939 Email mnps@bom7.vsnl.net.in

For group visits, prior confirmation recommended

PIROJSHANAGAR Vivek Kulkarni at Mangrove Project Office. Tel 55962075 Or Laxmikant Deshpande Tel 55962077

SANJAY GANDHI NATIONAL PARK Deputy Conservator of Forests, SGNP, Borivli (East), Mumbai 400 066. Tel 28860362, 28860389. For restricted areas, special permission needed from park's site office

SPECIES LISTING

The following species are representative of specific habitats, and though this may not be a comprehensive list, it includes those that are widespread. It does not imply that every species mentioned occurs at all sites of a habitat type. Common English names have been used where possible; elsewhere popular local names and the occasional scientific name are provided. Flora has been categorized as trees (woody plants, usually 2.5 m or more in height); shrubs and herbs that include seasonal plants; and species that have attributes of palms, bamboos, creepers or climbers.

FOREST
These sites include neighbouring edge-of-forest, scrub and grass, and waterside habitats

FLORA
Trees Teak, Kusum, Flame of the Forest, Red Silk Cotton, Yellow Silk Cotton, Indian Laburnum, Indian Coral, Haldu, Karanj, Black Plum (Jamun), Karaya, Kain, Wild Guava, Bonfire Tree, *Dillenia pentagyna*, Black Siris, White Siris, Ain, Asoka, Asana, Anjan, Rosewood, Sandpaper Tree, Variegated Bauhinia, Gela, Sacred Barna, Belleric Myrobalan, Amla, Gamari, Wodier Wood, Mango, Indian Medlar, Indian Kino, Indian Elm, Queen's Flower, Stripping Lady, Kakad, Tree of Damocles, Pala Indigo, Pula, Easter Tree, Pipal, Banyan, Country Fig (Gular), Dhaura, Coromandel Ebony, Butter Tree (Mahua), Macaranga, Dhaman, Phalsa, Spotted Gliricidia, Indian Nettle Tree, Rough-leaved Fig, Soccerball Tree

Shrubs & Herbs Hill Banana, Leea, Karvi, Christ's Thorn, Hedge Caper, Giant Milkweed, Fireflame Bush, Screw Fruit Bush, Blue Eranthemum, Blue Fountain Bush, Spiral Ginger, Common Balsam, Pin-cushion, Sensitive Smithia, Forest Barleria, Pink-striped Trumpet Lily, Indian Borage, Forest Spider Lily, Oriental Sesame, Devil's Claw, Hill Turmeric, Dragon Stalk Yam, Common Mallow, Wild Ladies' Fingers, Grape-leaved Mallow, Silver Spiked Cockscomb, Hedge Glory, Castor Oil Plant, Bengal Jute, American Mint, Common Sida, Jungle Flame, Tangle Mat, Yellow-berried Nightshade, Mexican Poppy, Forest Ghost Flower, Common Lantana

Palms, Bamboos, Creepers & Climbers Toddy Palm, Solid Bamboo, Thorny Bamboo,

Glory Lily, Paper Flower Climber, Woolly Elephant Climber, Crab-eyed Creeper, Common Cowitch, Common Passion Flower, Butterfly Bean, Creeping Hemp, Forest Beanstalk, Silky Elephant Glory, Greater Glory, Red Star Glory, Indian Sweet Pea, Wild Moong, Common Swordbean

MAMMALS

Leopard, Toddy Cat, Small Indian Civet, Rusty-spotted Cat, Jungle Cat, Jackal, Striped Hyena, Sambar, Barking Deer, Spotted Deer, Mouse Deer, Indian Giant Squirrel, Common Langur, Bonnet Macaque, Rhesus Macaque, Common Mongoose, Wild Boar, Black-naped Hare, Striped Palm Squirrel, Flying Fox, Bearded Sheath-tailed Bat, Painted Bat, Common Shrew, Common Bandicoot **Uncommon** Indian Pangolin

BIRDS

Residents Grey Junglefowl, Red Spurfowl, Indian Peafowl, Painted Francolin, Jungle Bush Quail, Crested Serpent Eagle, Changeable Hawk-eagle, Honey Buzzard, Shikra, Brown Hawk Owl, Jungle Owlet, Night Heron, Cattle Egret, Lesser Whistling Duck, Emerald Dove, Yellow-footed Pigeon, Pompadour Pigeon, Spotted Dove, Alexandrine Parakeet, Plum-headed Parakeet, White-naped Woodpecker, Black-rumped Flameback, Heart-spotted Woodpecker, Rufous Woodpecker, Brown-headed Barbet, White-throated Kingfisher, Greater Coucal, Greater Racket-tailed Drongo, White-bellied Drongo, Black Drongo, Indian Grey Hornbill, White-rumped Shama, Malabar Whistling Thrush, Orange-headed Thrush, Black-hooded Oriole, Black-headed Cuckooshrike, Large Cuckooshrike, Scarlet Minivet, Blue-winged Leafbird, Golden-fronted Leafbird, Red-whiskered Bulbul, White-browed Bulbul, Common Iora, Indian Scimitar Babbler, Puff-throated Babbler, Brown-cheeked Fulvetta, Tawny-bellied Babbler, Grey-breasted Prinia, Plain-billed Flowerpecker, Thick-billed

Flowerpecker, Crimson Sunbird, Loten's Sunbird, Purple Sunbird, Scaly-breasted Munia, Chestnut-shouldered Petronia
Winter Migrants Osprey, Peregrine Falcon, White-eyed Buzzard, Booted Eagle, Imperial Eagle, Purple Heron, Grey Heron, Asian Openbill, Spot-billed Duck, Oriental Turtle-dove, Blue-capped Rock Thrush, Spangled Drongo, Ashy Drongo, Bronzed Drongo, Red-throated Flycatcher, Paradise Flycatcher, Verditer Flycatcher, Grey-headed Canary Flycatcher, Grasshopper Warbler, Greenish Warbler, Tickell's Leaf Warbler, Booted Warbler, Lesser Whitethroat Warbler, Forest Wagtail, Olive-backed Pipit, Common Rosefinch
Monsoon Visitors Oriental Dwarf Kingfisher, Pied Cuckoo, Common Hawk-cuckoo, Grey-bellied Cuckoo, Banded-bay Cuckoo, Drongo Cuckoo, Indian Cuckoo
Uncommon Amur Falcon, Besra, Long-legged Buzzard, Black Eagle, Great Hornbill, Lesser Adjutant, Darter, Black-naped Oriole, Ultramarine Flycatcher, Brown Fish Owl, Mottled Wood Owl, Eurasian Eagle Owl, Green Imperial Pigeon, Blue-faced Malkoha, Brown-capped Pygmy Woodpecker, Malabar Pied Hornbill, Malabar Grey Hornbill, Malabar Parakeet, Streak-throated Woodpecker, Malabar Trogon, Bar-winged Flycatcher-Shrike, Eurasian Blackbird, Plain Flowerpecker, Crimson-backed Sunbird

REPTILES

Spectacled Cobra, Russell's Viper, Bamboo Pit Viper, Saw-scaled Viper, Common Krait, Rock Python, Forsten's Cat Snake, Trinket Snake, Vine Snake, Common Wolf Snake, Checkered Keelback, Striped Keelback, Bronzeback Treesnake, Rat Snake, Bengal Monitor, Chameleon, Spotted Rock Gecko, Bark Gecko, Kollegal Ground Gecko, Dwarf Gecko, Deccan Banded Gecko, Brook's Gecko, Forest Calotes, Common Skink, Small Skink, Snake-skink, Fan-throated Lizard, Indian Garden Lizard

SAHYADRI HILLS
Includes mountain-top evergreen forest, adjoining plateaus, waterbodies and hill slopes

FLORA
Trees Anjan, Black Plum (Jamun), Pan Jambul, Pisa, Mango, Chebulic Myrobalan, Belleric Myrobalan, Embelic Myrobalan, Ironwood Tree, Asana, Sacred Barna, Indian Laburnum, Asoka, Indian Medlar, True Cinnamon Tree, Kokam, Devil's Tree, Kamala, Karanj, Rosewood, Soapnut Tree, Coromandel Ebony, Hirda, Jackfruit, Gular, Putranjiva, Pula, Sandpaper Tree, Dhaman, Eucalyptus, Flame of the Forest, Red Silk Cotton, Indian Coral, Champak, Burma Ironwood, Indian Willow, Common Emetic Nut, Butter Tree (Mahua), Silver Oak, Chittagong Wood
Shrubs & Herbs Karvi, Hill Banana, Hill Turmeric, Dragon Stalk Yam, Indian Arrowroot, Firebush, Greater Rattle Pod, Ceylon Caper, Common Begonia, Violet Asytasia, Forest Spider Lily, Hill Justicia, Blue Fountain Bush, Reticulated Bladderwort, Bearded Marsh Star, Woodrow's Grape Tree, Common Hill Borage, False Guava, Fish-poison Bush, Konkan Pinda, Persian Mallow, Graham's Groundsel, Common Begonia, Dalzell's Yellow Balsam, Dalzell's Frerea, Rock Balsam, Common Balsam, Hill Balsam, Common Fox-tail Orchid, Long-tailed Habenaria, Blood Flower, Forest Flytrap, Violet Asytasia, Bombay Bean, Dhobi's Kerchief, Serpent Root, Blood Flower
Palms, Bamboos, Creepers & Climbers Solid Bamboo, Thorny Bamboo, Paper Flower Climber, Woolly Elephant Climber, Creeping Hemp, Common Passion Flower, Forest Beanstalk, Indian Sweet Pea, Flaming Spike Climber, Forest Flytrap, Bristle Gourd, Camel's Foot Climber, Common Forest Thunbergia, Deccan Clematis, Purple Heart Glory, Little Glory, Glory Lily

MAMMALS
Leopard, Small Indian Civet, Toddy Cat, Sambar, Spotted Deer, Mouse Deer, Barking Deer, Indian Porcupine, Indian Giant Squirrel, Common Mongoose, Black-naped Hare, Wild Boar, Eastern Horse-shoe Bat, Painted Bat

BIRDS
Residents Grey Junglefowl, Red Spurfowl, Blue-breasted Quail, Painted Francolin, Jungle Bush Quail, Black Eagle, Changeable Hawk-eagle, Bonelli's Hawk-eagle, Crested Serpent Eagle, Shikra, Peregrine (Shaheen) Falcon, Common Kestrel, Long-billed Vulture, White-rumped Vulture, Eurasian Eagle Owl, Brown Hawk Owl, Jungle Owlet, Collared Scops Owl, Grey Nightjar, Greater Coucal, Blue-faced Malkoha, Nilgiri Wood Pigeon, Green Imperial Pigeon, Emerald Dove, Pompadour Pigeon, Oriental Turtle Dove, Oriental Dwarf Kingfisher, Indian Grey Hornbill, Malabar Grey Hornbill, Malabar Pied Hornbill, Streak-throated Woodpecker, Heart-spotted Woodpecker, Alpine Swift, Malabar Trogon, Spangled Drongo, Bronzed Drongo, Greater Racket-tailed Drongo, Rufous Treepie, Scarlet Minivet, Black-hooded Oriole, Golden-fronted Leafbird, White-browed Fantail, White-throated Fantail, White-bellied blue Flycatcher, Sykes Crested Lark, Pied Bushchat, White-rumped Shama, Eurasian Blackbird, Malabar Whistling Thrush, Orange-headed Ground Thrush, Yellow-browed Bulbul, Black Bulbul, Puff-throated Babbler, Brown-cheeked Fulvetta, Indian Scimitar Babbler, Great Tit, Plain Flowerpecker, Crimson-backed Sunbird, Purple Sunbird, Crimson Sunbird, Crested Bunting
Winter Migrants Lesser Spotted Eagle, Besra, Booted Eagle, Eurasian Hobby, Ashy Drongo, Grey-headed Canary Flycatcher, Paradise Flycatcher, Blue-capped Rock Thrush, Blue Rock Thrush, Greenish Warbler, Tickell's Leaf Warbler, Tytler's Leaf Warbler, Olive-backed Pipit, Forest Wagtail, Common Rosefinch
Monsoon Visitors Rain Quail, Yellow-legged Buttonquail, Grey-bellied Cuckoo, Banded

Bay Cuckoo, Common Hawk Cuckoo, Drongo Cuckoo
Waterside Slaty-legged Crake, Blue-breasted Crake, Greater Flamingo, Eurasian Spoonbill, Asian Openbill, Black Ibis, Black-headed Ibis, Glossy Ibis, Great Egret, Little Egret, Grey Heron, Purple Heron, Pintail, Garganey, Common Teal, Spot-billed Duck, Lesser Whistling Duck, Common Pochard, Red-wattled Lapwing, Black-winged Stilt, Little Ringed Plover, Kentish Plover, Whiskered Tern, Indian Skimmer, Black-bellied Tern, Common Redshank, Green Sandpiper, Pied Kingfisher, White-browed Wagtail, Yellow Wagtail, White Wagtail
Uncommon Black-crested Baza, Fairy Bluebird, Great Hornbill

REPTILES
Spectacled Cobra, Malabar Pit Viper, Bamboo Pit Viper, Rock Python, Large-scaled Shieldtail, Beddome's Keelback, Ornate Flying Snake, Forsten's Cat Snake, Slender Coral Snake, Common Wolf Snake, Bengal Monitor, Spotted Rock Gecko, Deccan Banded Gecko, Forest Calotes

COAST & WETLAND

Includes coastal, creek-side, estuarine, and inland lake and marsh habitats, some in urban areas

FLORA

Trees Australian Acacia, Babul, Su-babul, Indian Jujube (Ber), Neem, Tamarind, Black Plum (Jamun), Baobab, Indian Almond, Rain Tree, Portia Tree, Indian Laburnum, Copper Pod, Flamboyant (Gulmohur), Banyan, Pipal, Manila Tamarind, Bellyache Plant, Yellow Oleander, Mango, Karanj, Pala Indigo
Mangrove Vegetation White Mangrove, Grey Mangrove, Mangrove Apple, Toothbrush Plant, Orange Mangrove, Red Mangrove, Sea Holly, Mangrove Fern, River Mangrove, Common Indian Saltwort, Spur Mangrove, Milky Mangrove, Shore Purselane, Mangrove Beanstalk, Common Hedge Bower
Shrubs & Herbs Devil's Claw, Oriental Sesame, Bengal Jute, Glory Lily, Marsh Glory, Water Hyacinth, Water Lettuce, Castor Oil Plant, Hedge Glory, Screw Fruit Bush, Dragon Stalk Yam, Common Mallow, Wild Ladies' Fingers, Grape-leaved Mallow, Marsh Barbel, Common Marsh Buckwheat, Christ's Thorn, Indian Water Lily, Indian Lotus, Star Water Lily
Palms, Bamboos, Creepers & Climbers Toddy Palm, Coconut Palm, Wild Date Palm, Fish-tail Palm, Marsh Glory, Bank Mat

MAMMALS

Jackal, Wild Boar, Black-naped Hare, Indian Porcupine, Flying Fox, Short-nosed Fruit Bat
Uncommon Leopard, Jungle Cat

BIRDS

Residents White-bellied Sea Eagle, Brahminy Kite, Barn Owl, Greater Painted Snipe, Purple Swamphen, White-breasted Waterhen, Yellow Bittern, Cinnamon Bittern, Ruddy-breasted Crake, Blue-breasted Rail, Pheasant-tailed Jacana, Bronze-winged Jacana, Red-wattled Lapwing, Little Cormorant, Indian Cormorant, Cattle Egret, Little Egret, Intermediate Egret, Little Green Heron, Night Heron, White-throated Kingfisher, White-eared Bulbul, Clamorous Reed Warbler, Zitting Cisticola, Plain Prinia, Grey-breasted Prinia, Black-throated Weaver, Baya Weaver, Scaly-breasted Munia, White-rumped Munia, Indian Silverbill, Black-headed Munia
Winter Migrants Osprey, Imperial Eagle, Greater Spotted Eagle, Tawny Eagle, Peregrine Falcon, Laggar Falcon, Common Kestrel, Eurasian Marsh Harrier, Pallid Harrier, Hen Harrier, Short-eared Owl, Greater Flamingo, Lesser Flamingo, Asian Openbill, Painted Stork, Glossy Ibis, Grey Heron, Purple Heron, Pied Avocet, Bar-tailed Godwit, Black-tailed Godwit, Eurasian Oystercatcher, Ruddy Turnstone, Eurasian Curlew, Whimbrel,

Curlew Sandpiper, Dunlin, Common Snipe, Fantail Snipe, Black-winged Stilt, Common Redshank, Greenshank, Ruff, Green Sandpiper, Spotted Sandpiper, Grey Plover, Golden Plover, Kentish Plover, Little Ringed Plover, Pallas's Gull, Heuglin's Gull, Great Black-headed Gull, Brown-headed Gull, Little Stint, Temminck's Stint, Gull-billed Tern, Little Tern, Whiskered Tern, Caspian Tern, Black-capped Kingfisher, Blue-tailed Bee-eater, Bluethroat, Lesser Whitethroat
Uncommon White Stork, Crab Plover

REPTILES
Glossy Marsh Snake, Dog-faced Water Snake, Common Wolf Snake, Checkered Keelback, Spectacled Cobra, Russell's Viper, Saw-scaled Viper, Chittul, Rat Snake, Banded Racer, Banded Kukri, Bengal Monitor, Common Skink, Snake Skink

SCRUB & GRASS
Most rapidly expanding habitat; flora and, consequently, fauna display a strong human influence

FLORA
Trees Mango, Black Plum, Tamarind, Indian Almond, Pipal, Banyan, Neem, Country Fig (Umber), Red Silk Cotton, Indian Coral, Australian Acacia, Babul, Su-babul, Indian Jujube, Flame of the Forest, Portia Tree, Karanj, Bonfire Tree, Karaya, Baobab, Teak, Kusum, Yellow Oleander, Casuarina, Indian Laburnum, Copper Pod, Mast Tree, Drumstick Tree, Indian Cork Tree, Cashewnut, Flamboyant (Gulmohur), Manila Tamarind, Butter tree (Mahua), Spotted Gliricidia, Indian Nettle Tree, Vilayati Babul
Shrubs & Herbs Leea, Christ's Thorn, Bellyache Plant, Marsh Glory, Hedge Glory, Castor, Oriental Sesame, Bengal Jute, Hedge Caper, Giant Milkweed, Common Lantana, Common Mallow, Wild Ladies' Fingers, Screw-fruit Bush, Blue Eranthemum, Blue Fountain Bush, Spiral Ginger, Common Balsam, Pin-cushion, Sensitive Smithia, Indian Borage, Congress Grass, Oriental Sesame, Devil's Claw, Hill Turmeric, Dragon Stalk Yam, Grape-leaved Mallow, Silver Spiked Cockscomb, Common Swordbean, Castor Oil Plant, American Mint, Common Sida, Jungle Flame, Tangle Mat, Common Sorrel, Yellow-berried Nightshade, Mexican Poppy, Forest Ghost Flower.
Palms, Bamboos, Creepers & Climbers Toddy Palm, Coconut Palm, Wild Date Palm, Fish-tail Palm, Branching Palm, Solid Bamboo, Thorny Bamboo, Glory Lily, Crab-eyed Creeper, Common Cowitch, Ivy Gourd, Purple Trumpet, Common Passion Flower, Railway Glory, Red Star Glory, Blue Dawn Glory, Common Night Glory

MAMMALS
Jackal, Striped Hyena, Jungle Cat, Wild Boar, Black-naped Hare, Indian Porcupine, Flying Fox, Short-nosed Fruit Bat
Uncommon Leopard

BIRDS
Residents Jungle Bush Quail, Barred Buttonquail, Barn Owl, Indian Nightjar, Grey Nightjar, Red-wattled Lapwing, Spotted Dove, Laughing Dove, Rose-ringed Parakeet, Alexandrine Parakeet, Asian Palm Swift, White-throated Kingfisher, Green Bee-eater, Coppersmith Barbet, Rufous-tailed Lark, Ashy-crowned Sparrow Lark, Oriental Skylark, Malabar Crested Lark, Paddyfield Pipit, Dusky Crag Martin, Red-rumped Swallow, Wire-tailed Swallow, Black Drongo, Asian Pied Starling, Common Myna, Common Iora, Red-whiskered Bulbul, Red-vented Bulbul, White-browed Bulbul, Yellow-eyed Babbler, White-throated Babbler, Jungle Babbler, Tickell's Blue Flycatcher, White-throated Fantail, White-browed Fantail, Common Tailorbird, Ashy Prinia, Grey-breasted Prinia, Plain Prinia, Zitting Cisticola, Indian Robin, Magpie Robin,

Purple-rumped Sunbird, Purple Sunbird, Baya Weaver, Black-throated Weaver, Indian Silverbill, Scaly-breasted Munia, Black-headed Munia, Red Avadavat, Chestnut-shouldered Petronia

Winter Migrants White-eyed Buzzard, Booted Eagle, Imperial Eagle, Tawny Eagle, Steppe Eagle, Black-shouldered Kite, Pallid Harrier, Montagu's Harrier, Hen Harrier, Common Kestrel, Peregrine Falcon, Laggar Falcon, Blue-tailed Bee-eater, Indian Roller, Common Hoopoe, Eurasian Wryneck, Greater Short-toed Lark, Barn Swallow, Long-tailed Shrike, Brown Shrike, Rufous-tailed Shrike, Bay-backed Shrike, Rosy Starling, Chestnut-tailed Starling, Red-throated Flycatcher, Booted Warbler, Grasshopper Warbler, Blyth's Reed Warbler, Lesser Whitethroat, Common Stonechat, Desert Wheatear, Pied Bushchat, Black Redstart, Citrine Wagtail, White Wagtail, Black-headed Bunting, Red-headed Bunting

Uncommon Grey Francolin, Pied Harrier, Lesser Kestrel, Savanna Nightjar, Yellow-wattled Lapwing, Blue-cheeked Bee-eater, Ashy-wood Swallow, Isabelline Wheatear

URBAN

Includes scrub, light forest, coastal and creek-side habitats within Greater Mumbai and Thane

FLORA

Trees Pipal, Banyan, Tamarind, Putranjiva, Manila Tamarind, Indian Cork Tree, Kapok, Red Silk Cotton, Yellow Silk Cotton, Flamboyant (Gulmohur), Copper Pod, Plumeria, Indian Coral, Neem, Mast Tree, Black Plum (Jamun), Mango, Indian Jujube, Rain Tree, Indian Almond, African Tulip Tree, Cannonball Tree, Australian Acacia, Indian Kino, Queen's Flower, Yellow Oleander, Cashewnut, Bonfire Tree, Jackfruit, *Barringtonia*, Coral Jasmine, Sacred Barna, Portia Tree, Su-babul, Flame of the Forest, Easter Tree, Drumstick Tree, Ironwood Tree, Casuarina, Teak, Rubber Tree, Custard Apple, Eucalyptus, Bottlebrush Tree, Indian Nettle Tree, Singapore Cherry, Rough-leaved Fig, Coralwood, Fern Tree

Shrubs & Herbs Leea, Castor Oil Plant, Christ's Thorn, Hedge Caper, Brazil Jute, Candle Cassia, Common Lantana, Wild Ladies' Fingers, Passion Flower, Giant Milkweed, Common Balsam, Spiral Ginger, Pin-cushion, Indian Borage, Hedge Glory, Castor, Country Mallow, American Mint, Common Sida, Common Sorrel, Yellow-berried Nightshade, Mexican Poppy

Palms, Bamboos, Creepers & Climbers Cycas, Toddy Palm, Coconut Palm, Date Palm, Bottle Palm, Fish-tail Palm, Traveller's Palm, Areca Palm, Thorny Bamboo, Golden Bamboo, Railway Glory, Blue Dawn Glory, Glory Lily, Crab-eyed Creeper, Indian Sweet Pea, Common Cowitch, Common Passion Flower, Ivy Gourd

MAMMALS

Leopard, Jackal, Bonnet Macaque, Flying Fox, Fulvous Fruit Bat, Short-nosed Fruit Bat, Indian Pipistrelle, Striped Palm Squirrel

BIRDS

Peregrine Falcon, Brahminy Kite, Shikra, Barn Owl, Spotted Owlet, Cattle Egret, Pond Heron, Ring-necked Parakeet, Alexandrine Parakeet, White-throated Kingfisher, Pied Cuckoo, Greater Coucal, Koel, Green Bee-eater, Coppersmith Barbet, Spotted Dove, Long-tailed Shrike, Golden Oriole, Common Iora, Common Hoopoe, House Swift, Palm Swift, Red-rumped Swallow, Barn Swallow, Red-vented Bulbul, Common Myna, Chestnut-tailed Starling, Pied Starling, White-throated Fantail, Paradise Flycatcher, Red-throated Flycatcher, Magpie Robin, Tailorbird, Ashy Prinia, Grey-breasted Prinia, Purple-rumped Sunbird, Purple Sunbird, Pale-billed Flowerpecker, Grey Wagtail, Yellow

Wagtail, Indian Silverbill

REPTILES
Spectacled Cobra, Russell's Viper, Common Krait, Glossy Marsh Snake, Dog-faced Water Snake, Common Wolf Snake, Striped Keelback, Checkered Keelback, Bronzeback Snake, Rat Snake, Common Kukri, Chameleon, Garden Lizard, Forest Calotes, Southern House Gecko, Common Skink, Bengal Monitor

MUMBAI'S GREEN HERITAGE

Several sites in Mumbai are popularly known by their original flora which, in many instances, is no longer to be seen.

Tamarind Lane: from a tamarind grove
Parel: from *paral*, the Trumpet Flower Tree
Wadala: from a *vad* or banyan grove
Worli: corruption of *vad-ali*, or Banyan trees
Cumballa Hill: named after *kambal* or lotus
Umerkhadi: a creek lined with fig trees
Bhendi Bazaar: from the Portia tree (*bhendi*)
Fanaswadi: named after jackfruit
Tardeo: from the *taad* (Palmyra)
Madmallah: from *maad* or Coconut Palm
Byculla: from the *bhaya* tree (*Cassia fistula*)
Babulnath: from a plantation of Babul

Laburnum Road: lined by Indian Laburnum
Gulmohar Road: from the Gulmohur (Flamboyant) tree
Kelewadi: plantain grove
Borivli: from the *bora* tree (Indian Jujube)
Bori Bandar: from the *bora* tree (Indian Jujube)
Matheran: 'forest on the forehead'
Palasdhari: from *palash* or Flame of the Forest tree
Asangaon: from the *asana* tree (*Bridellia retusa*)

SOME RARE TREES IN MUMBAI

American Sumach *Caesalpinia coriaria* Veermata Jijabai Bhonsle Udyan (Byculla Zoo), Thane
Australian Chestnut *Castanospermum australe* Garden near Mantralaya, Byculla Zoo
Branching Palm *Hyphaene* species BPT Hospital in Wadala, Dadar Parsi Colony, Hanging Gardens, Godrej Baug, Bhandup
Brazilian Rusty Pod *Peltophorum linnaei* Thane, Kisan Nagar, Byculla Zoo
Calabash Tree *Cresentia cujete* Byculla Zoo, Khopoli power station, en route to Chinchoti
Dikamali *Gardenai resinifera* Talzan, SGNP, CEC in Goregaon
Elephant's Ear Pod Tree *Enterolobium cyclocarpum* JK Gram in Thane, Kamala Nehru Park
Fern Tree *Filicum decipiens* Hanging Gardens, Byculla Zoo, near Haji Ali

Flame Amherstia or Pride of Burma
Amherstia nobilis Mumbai University Gardens (Fort), Byculla Zoo, Thane industrial area
Hoom *Mitusa tomentosa* CEC, SGNP
Horse Cassia *Cassia grandis* Ciba Geigy Research Centre in Goregaon, Thane, Byculla Zoo
Kamala *Mallotus philippensis* Film City Road, Thane, Mumbra hills, Yeur
Kesri *Bixa oreollana* Byculla Zoo, Bhavan's College campus in Andheri
Kleinhovia *Kleinhovia hospita* Byculla Zoo, near Andheri station, Dadar Parsi Colony, Horniman Circle garden, Parel sports ground
Krishna's Buttercup *Ficus krishnae* Byculla Zoo, Maharashtra National Park, Ciba Geigy Research Centre in Goregaon
Lampeti *Duabanga grandiflora* Gandhi Smarak, SGNP, Aarey Colony

Loquat *Eriobotrya japonica* near Sion Circle
Motha Kamal *Dillenia indica* Byculla Zoo,
Malabar Hill, Sagar Upwan in Colaba, along
Thane-Belapur Road
Padal *Stereospermum chelonoides* Ambedkar
Garden in Powai, near Kurla station, Morarjee
Mills in Lalbaug
Pink Cassia *Cassia renigera* Horniman Circle
garden, Badhwar Park, Navi Mumbai
Red Sandalwood *Pterocarpus santalinus*
Byculla Zoo
Rudraksha *Elaeocarpus sphaericus* Byculla
Zoo, DC bungalow in Thane
Sandalwood *Santalum album* Ruia College,
Thane, Phansad
Seaside Grape *Coccoloba uvifera* Sagar
Upwan in Colaba, Thane

Star Apple Tree *Chrysophyllum cainito*
Mumbai University Garden in Fort, Kala
Ghoda, Byculla Zoo, KEM Hospital
compound, near Hutatma Chowk, SEEPZ in
Andheri
Talipot Palm *Corypha umbraculifera* Byculla
Zoo, Khareghat Colony (near Hanging
Gardens)
Tolu Balsam Tree *Myroxylon balsamina*
Malabar Hill, Mahim-Matunga, Pirojshanagar
Trincomali Wood *Berrya cordifolia* Byculla
Zoo, Malabar Hill
Undi *Calophyllum inophyllum* Aksa, Byculla
Zoo
Yellow Silk Cotton *Cochlospermum religiosum*
TIFR and Sagar Upwan in Colaba, CEC,
Talzan, Maharashtra National Park

THE BAOBAB

The enormous Baobab (*Adansonia digitata*),
which has one of the longest life-spans of any
living organism, is popularly known as *gorakh
chinch*. Arab traders of Mughal times are
believed to have introduced the tree to India
from its native Africa, and it was
subsequently spread extensively by the
Portuguese. It may have an even more
ancient connection with India, as a sculpture
in the Ellora caves depicts Indrani seated
below what could well be a Baobab tree.
Specimens of this tree can be seen in several
spots in Mumbai.

Navy Nagar (including a very large one on
N Moos Road): 6, **TIFR campus**: 1, **Byculla
Zoo**: 3, **Chhatrapati Shivaji Maharaj Vastu
Sanghralaya** (Prince of Wales Museum)
grounds: 1, **St Xavier's School** (Dhobi Talao):
1, **Near Azad Maidan police station**: 1,

Mumbai University campus (Fort): 1,
Shankar Lane (Kandivli West): 1, **Near SV
Road** (Santa Cruz West): 1, **junction of
Station Road and SV Road** (Ville Parle West):
1, **SEEPZ area**: several, **Opposite Bhabha
Hospital** (Bandra West): 1, **Kisan Nagar**
(Thane): 3, **SK Bole Road**: 1, **Mandala
Colony**: 1, **Sewri**: 1, **Kokarli** (on Agardanda
Road): 12 or more, **Near Vahal village** (on
main road from CBD-Belapur to Jasai, *c.* 4.5
km off the Palm Beach junction): 6, **Mora
village** (off Uran): 3, **Alibaug-Kihim Road**: 1,
Near Revdanda (Alibaug-Murud Road): 1,
near Marol Road: 1, **Marve and Madh
Roads**: 4, **Near Manori village**: 1,
Ghodbunder (near Fort and MTDC lodge): 5
large, **Bassein Fort area**: 6 large, **INS Hamla
grounds**: 1, **Parsi Colony** (Dadar): 1, **Gorai**:
1, **Ciba Geigy campus** (Goregaon East): 1,
Maharashtra National Park: 1 newly planted

CONVERSIONS *to metric system*

1 inch   2.542 centimeters (cm)
1 foot   0.305 metres (m)

1 mile   1.609 kilometers (km)
1 acre   0.405 hectares (ha)

CREDITS

DR B DASGUPTA 24 *right*
BHARATH RAMAMRUTHAM 23 *bottom*, 37,
DEEPAK CHACHRA Maps, inside front cover, 20,
36, 39, 41, 45, 49, 54, 64, 69, 91, 96,
101, 104, 106, 112, 119, 122
DIGANT DESAI 31 *2nd from top*, 42, 43 *top*, 44,
73 *top*, 101.
GV AJAY 77 *bottom*
ISSAC KEHIMKAR 38 *top*,
KRUPAKAR-SENANI Cover, 22 *top*, 27 *bottom*, 31
top, 41, 43 *2nd from top*, 47 *bottom*, 50

top, 53 *top*, 64, 65 *top*, 95 *top*, 120 *bottom*
NAYAN-MAHESH 4, 35 *2nd from top*, 38 *bottom*,
50 *3rd from top*, 56 *top right*, 59 *top*, 61
top, 73 *bottom and 3rd from top*, 78 *3rd
from top*, 81 *top*, 83 *top*, 85 *centre*, 88 *top*,
92 *top*, 100, 103 *top*, 106 *top*, 107 *top*,
110, 117 *top*
RISHI BAJPAI 112 *bottom*
V MUTHURAMAN 38 *centre*
VIVEK SINHA 26 top, 123 *bottom*
THAKUR DALIP SINGH 88 *centre*

ACKNOWLEDGEMENTS

This book has been made possible by the support of Deutsche Bank that has always attached great importance to environment. I especially thank Pavan Sukhdev and Dawn Milne for their wholehearted support.

My family continues to tolerate the eccentricities of a compulsive nature-enthusiast, much to my surprise. I dedicate this work to my parents, wife and little Yuhina, and to the late Humayun Abdulali and JS Serrao, passionate naturalists with whom my pal Joslin and I spent many years exploring the region.

I owe a great debt to many individuals who generously helped with this book. Deepak Chachra went out of his way, patiently toiling on the invaluable maps. Sanal Nair, Dr Salil Choksi, Aadesh Shivkar and Nayan Khanolkar for continual support. Dr MR Almeida and Dr Rajendra Shinde for abundant help on flora. Isaac Kehimkar, Naresh Chaturvedi, Varad Giri, Deepak Apte and Amit Chavan at BNHS for fascinating insights. Vivek Kulkarni of Godrej Mangrove Project for valuable inputs. Mahrukh Bulsara for help collecting useful data.

Among many naturalist-colleagues, I thank Dr Neil Soares, Vinod Haritwal, Digant Desai, Celine Anthony, Vijay Awsare,

Anil Pinto, Kedar Bhide, Nitin Jamdar, Kiran Srivastav, Rishad Naoroji, Leon Lobo, Dr Parvish Pandya, Debi Goenka, Pravin Choudhry, Amogh Ghaisas, Amar Deshpande, Sagar Mhatre, Sunetro Ghosal, Manisha Shah, and last but not least, Capt Kevin Paul and Cletus D'Souza. Mr Ratan Lalkaka, HK Divekar and KB Singh helped with information on several sites.

Officials of Maharashtra forest/wildlife departments at Mumbai, Thane, Tansa and Phansad have been tremendous help and those of CFRI, BMC, MbPT and JNPT were always cooperative.

My never-complaining, sturdy Ford Ikon played a central role. She effortlessly negotiated every hurdle over 10,000 trouble-free kilometers, helping explore, discover what might have otherwise been just 'heard-about'. The *Eicher Mumbai City Map* and Harish Kapadia's *Trek the Sahyadris* were tremendously useful references.

Finally, the very professional IBH team. Padmini, Meera, Lavanya, Shikha, Jatin and Lucy helped crystallize a clutter of ideas and scribbles into a sensible book. Any errors are entirely my work.

SUNJOY MONGA
2nd December, 2003

INDEX *Page numbers in bold refer to illustrations*

ANIMAL KINGDOM

Adjutant, Lesser, 20
Ant, Harvester: nests, **24**
Avocet, 101, 108; Pied, 109
Babbler, 26, 35, 45, 63, 71, 73, 79, 107: Common, 80, 96; Jungle, 67; Large Grey, 71; Puff-throated, **65**; Scimitar, 36; White-throated, 79; Yellow-eyed, 83, 95
Barbet, 29, 70, 112: Brown-headed, 46; Coppersmith, 119, 121
Bats, 128: Bearded Sheath-tailed, 38, 66; Flying Fox, 38, 125, 127; Fruit **13**; Fulvous Fruit, 66; Short-nosed Fruit, 125, 127
Baya, **111**: nest, **81**,
Baza, Black-crested, 73
Bee-eater, 33, 39, 56, 71, 77, 96, 105, **112**, 113,126: Green, 67, 114
Beetles, 33, **43**, 50, 68, 73; Blister, 83; Whirligig, 74
Bittern, 87, 96: Black, 107; Cinnamon, **33**, 59, 85; Yellow, 104
Blackbirds, 60: Eurasian, 47
Bluebird, Fairy, 73
Bluethroat, 91, 95, 104, 107
Boar, Wild, 19, 20, 27, 33, 50, 58, 74, 78
Booby, Masked, 92, 114
Bugs, 33, 50, 68, 73
Bulbul, 26, 33, **43**, 45, 63, 70, 73, 77, 79, 95, 96, 97, 113, 116, 119, 121, 128: Black, 60, 74; Bluethroat, 104; Red-vented, **122**, 125; White-eared, 96, 104, 107; Yellow-browed, 74
Bunting, 71: Black-headed, 33, 108; Crested, 71
Butterflies, 8, 18, 76, 78, 83, 85, 99, 117, 124, 126, 127: Blue Mormon, 50, 68; Blue Pansy, 82; Common Blue Bottle, **23**; Crimson Rose, 82; Great Eggfly, 82; Lemon Pansy, **119**; Map, 73; Peacock Pansy, **78**; Spots Swordtail, 15, **35**; Yam fly, **25**
Buttonquail, 69: Barred, 59, 80, 92; Yellow-legged, **70**
Buzzard, 54: Honey, 50, 74; White-eyed, 35

Calotes, Forest, 15, **36**
Cat: Jungle, 53, 59, 81, 83, 90, 93, 95, 96, 106, 107, 117; Rusty Spotted, 29, 36, 45; Toddy, 63, 85
Chat, 35, 70, 71, 105; Pied Bush, 67
Chital. See Deer, Spotted
Cicadas, 15, 45, 46
Civet, 27, 68, **69**, 74: Common Palm, 22, 29, 58, 59, 77; Small Indian, 19, 36, 41, 45, 49, 50, 69, 72, 73
Cobra: Indian, 19; Spectacled, 81, 124
Cormorant, 39, 52, 70, 94, 118, 124: Great, 23, 84
Coucal, Greater, 88, 92, 119, 125
Crab, 26, **67**, 70, 87, 96, 104, 120: Fiddler, 15, 38, 94; Hermit, 38; Mumbai species, 11
Crake, 59, 69
Crocodile, 23. *See also* Mugger
Crow, House, 79, 92
Crustaceans, 15, 38, 101, 103
Cuckoo, 15, 31, 35, 36, 41, 53, 69, 95, 107, 112: Pied, 79
Curlew, 82, 101, 112: Stone, 111
Deer, 36: Barking, 14, 18, 19, 26, 36, 47, 48, 49, 50, 58, 59, 69, 74; Mouse, 18, 19, 48, 49, 74; Spotted, 14, 18, 19, 20, 23, 48, 50. *See also* Sambar
Dhole, 40
Dolphin, 11
Dove, 70, 71, 77, 79, 95, 96, 105, 106, 111, 116: Emerald, 25, 49; Laughing, 80; Spotted, **53**, 67, 92
Dragonfly, **112**, **117**
Drongo, 21, 29, 45, 47, 53, 70, 77, 78, 79, 95, 116: Ashy, 47, 119; Bronzed, 47; Greater Racket-tailed, 21, 26, **41**, 46; Spangled, 22, 25; White-bellied, 33, 39
Duck, 41: Comb, 85, 98, **99**; Lesser Whistling, 56, 78, 84, 91, 118; Spot-billed, 98; Whistling, 20
Dunlin, 101
Eagle, 54, 74: *Aquila*, 78, 87, 94, 103, 104; Black, 64; Booted, 53, 55; Crested Serpent, 30, **31**, 71; Grey-headed Fish, 20; Imperial, 80, 87, 100; Short-toed, 33, 53, 87, 100, 107;

Steppe, 80; White-bellied Sea, 13, 27, 38, 92, 100, 104, **110**, 112, 114
Egret, 94, 118, 124: Cattle, 93; Reef, 112; Western Reef, 38
Falcon, 54, 57, 65, 104, 105: Amur, 20; Laggar, 107; Peregrine, 10, 23, 31, 43, 60, 71, 74, 92, 95, 100
Fantail, 116: White-browed, 110; White-spotted, 88; White-throated, 92, 104, 125
Fish species, 8, 11; trade, 11
Flameback, Black-rumped, 33, 39, 88
Flamingo, 15, 92, 104, 105, 106, 108: Greater, 38, 70, 101; Lesser, 38, 97, 101
Flowerpecker, 113
Fly, Robber, **31**
Flycatcher, 21, 26, 36, 45, 47, 63, 77, 95, 97, 112, 113: Grey-headed Canary, 49-50; Paradise, 39, 88, 94, 110, 119, **123**, 125, 128; Ultramarine, 73; Verditer, 39, 47, 49; White-bellied Blue, 73, 74
Flycatcher-shrike, Bar-winged, 49
Flying Fox, 38, 125, 127
Francolin, 35, 41, 56, 100: Grey, 100; Painted, 36, 55, 100
Frigatebird, Lesser, 114
Frog, 45, **67**, 68, 69, 81, 86, 87: Common Bull, 83; Fungoid, 19, 24, 47, **50**; Indian Bull, 47; Ornate Narrow-mouthed, 24, 47; Short-headed Burrowing, 24
Fulvetta, Brown-cheeked, 24, 30
Garganey, 33, 41, 70, 84, 98, 106
Gastropod species, 11
Gaur, 40, 63, 64
Geckos, **87**, 88: Rock, 66, 86, 113
Godwit, 101, 108, 109
Goose, Greylag, 96
Grassbird, Broad-tailed, 61
Grasshopper, 33, 73, **121**, 126: Hooded, **78**; long-horned, 77; Painted, **33**; short-horned, 76
Grebe, Little, 52, 79, 111
Gull, 38, 86, 92, 93, 97, 100, 101, **103**, 104, 106, 113, 114: Black-headed, 109; Heuglin's, 99; Pallas's, 38, 99; Slender-billed, 109, 112
Hare, 55; Black-naped, 23, 28, 33, 35, 57, 74

Harrier, 33, 56, 111: Hen, 107;
  Marsh, 56, 87, 107, 118, 124,
  126; Pallid, 113; Pied, 80
Hawk, Shikra, 56, 110, 116, 119
Hawkmoth: Death's Head, 68;
  Olive Green, 35
Heron, 38, 39, 70, 100, **106**,
  108, 112, 113, 114, 118, 124:
  Grey, 104, 106, 123; Indian
  Pond, **92**; Little, 104; Night,
  20, 125; Purple, **14**
Heronries, 90, 106, 107, 121
Hobby, Eurasian, 19
Hoopoe, 92, 112, 113
Hornbill, 50: Great, 19; Grey, 95;
  Indian Grey, 15, 114; Malabar
  Grey, 73, 74; Malabar Pied,
  19, 50, 61
Hyena, Striped, 28, 33, 41, 45,
  53, 54, 69, 77, 106
Ibis, 105, 106, 108: Black-headed,
  85; Glossy, 85, 98, 118
Iora, 95, 97, 116
Jacana, 108, 112; Bronze-winged,
  79, **85**; Pheasant-tailed, 79
Jackal *in*: coastal & wet areas, 90,
  91, 92, 93, 95, 96, 105, 107;
  forests, 28, 33; Sahyadri, 53,
  54, 55, 57, 69; scrub & grass,
  77, 81, 83, 85, 86; urban
  areas, 117, 124
Junglefowl, 45, 50: Grey, 26, 33, 73
Keelback, 81; Checkered, 27, 55
Kestrel, 10, 59, **65**, 70: Common,
  31, 33, 43, 65, 71, 74, 87,
  113; Lesser, 83
Kingfisher, 38, 39, 100, 105, 112,
  114: Black-capped, 94, 112;
  White-throated, 15, **88**
Kite, 105: Black, 94, 104, 107,
  119; Black-eared, 35; Black-
  shouldered, 70, 87,107, 111,
  120; Brahminy, 53, **88**, 91, 107
Krait, Common, 81
Kukri, Common, 81
Ladybirds, 83
Langur, 23: Common, 33, 54, 63,
  66, 69
Lapwing, 56, 111: Yellow-
  wattled, 58, 93; Red-wattled,
  19, 92
Lark, 19, 33, 56, 70, 71, 82, 106,
  111, 120: Malabar Crested,
  87; Rufous-tailed, 87; Short-
  toed, 108
Leafbird, 29, 53, 70: Blue-winged,
  100
Leopard, 14, 16, 28, 29, 36, 41,
  47, 50, 77, 79: *in* SGNP, 18,

19, 20, 21, 23, 26, 27; *in*
  Sahyadri, 57, 58, 63, 72, 74;
  in urban areas, 119, 121
Lizards, 68, 73, 80, 113, 114
Locust, Coffee, 47
Macaque, Bonnet, 38, 63, 66
Malkoha: Blue-faced, 49; Sirkeer, 71
Martin, 59, 114: Crag, 96; Dusky
  Crag, 113
Minivet, 36: Ashy, 47; Scarlet, 30,
  39, **47**, **50**
Mites, Red Velvet, **35**
Molluscs, 38, 101, 103
Mongoose, 53, 54, 55, 77:
  Common, 18, 28, 33, 57, 79,
  81, 83, 85, 90, 92, 119, 124
Monitor, Bengal, 19, 33, 55, 59,
  79, 81, 84, 95, 96, 107, 117,
  119, 124
Moth, 66, 73: Atlas, **31**, 68;
  Moon, 68, **70**; Owl, 19; Silk,
  83; Tussor Silk, **83**
Mudskippers, 15, 26, 38, 94, 96,
  104
Mugger, 19, 118, 119
Munia, 120
Myna, Jungle, 108
Nightjar, 23, 35, 74: Common
  Indian, 96
Openbill, Asian, 85, 118
Oriole, 29, 73, 113, 128: Black-
  hooded, **27**, 33; Black-naped,
  19-20; Golden, 92, **95**, 119,
  121, 125, 126, 128
Osprey, 22, 27, 98, 104, 107
Owl: Barn, 128; Brown Fish, 20, 86;
  Eurasian Eagle, 25, **26**, 97, 111
Owlet, Spotted, 128
Oystercatcher, 38, 111, 112:
  Eurasian, 37
Pangolin, Indian, 72
Panther, Black, 63
Parakeet, 73: Alexandrine, 88;
  Malabar, 49, 74; Red-breasted,
  127; Vernal Hanging, 49
Pheasant, Crow, 116
Pigeon, 95: Green Imperial, 49,
  73; Nilgiri Wood, 61, 74;
  Pompadour, 46; Yellow-footed
  Green, 123
Pintail, 41, 52, 70, 98, 106:
  Northern, 33, 84
Pipit, 19, 106, 111
Plover, 101, 106: Crab, 94;
  Kentish, 70; Little Ringed, 70;
  Pacific Golden, 96
Pochard, Red-crested, 70
Porcupine, 53: Indian, 41
Porpoise, Finless Black, 11

Pratincole, 111: Oriental, 92
Prawns, 70, 120
Praying mantis, 26, 73, 76, 126
Primates, 36, 38. *See also* Langur;
  Macaque
Prinia, 77, 95: Ashy, 83; Plain, 83
Python, 55: Rock, 119
Quail, 31, 35, 41, 56, 77, 78, 79,
  95, 100, 112: Jungle Bush, 59,
  92, 107
Rails, 59, 69, 87, 96
Raptors, 36, 38, 53, 56, 78
Red Knot, 107
Redshank: Common, 107;
  Spotted, 108
Reptile species, 8
Robin: Indian, 92, 95; Magpie
  117, 125, 128
Rodents, 80, 81, 83, 127
Roller, 105: Indian, **35**, 67, 111
Rosefinch, Common, 47
Ruff, 107
Sambar, 14, **15**, 18, 19, 20, **22**,
  23, 27, 47, 48, 63, 74
Sandpiper, 101, 106, 109:
  Curlew, 87; Green, 124; Red-
  billed, 107; Spotted, 124
Scorpions, **61**, 66, 86
Shaheen. *See* Falcon, Peregrine
Shama, 30, 45, 46
Shark, Whale, 11
Shelduck, Ruddy, 108
Shikra, 56, 110, 116, 119
Shoveller, 70, 84
Shrike, 56, 70, 78, 105, 106,
  111, 113: Large Cuckoo, 100;
  Long-tailed, **78**, 107, 126
Silverbill, **81**
Skimmer, Indian, 70
Skylark, Oriental, **56**, 92
Snakes, 68, 73, 113: aquatic, 96,
  104; Banded Racer, 81;
  Common Kukri, 81; Common
  Rat, 124; Dog-faced Water,
  103; Glossy Marsh, 103; Rat,
  87, 107; Wolf, 81. *See also*
  Cobra; Keelback; Krait; Python;
  Treesnake; Vinesnake; Viper
Snipe, Greater Painted, **109**;
  Painted, 85
Spiders, 66, 73, 86, **87**; Catleg,
  73; Giant Wood, 47
Spoonbill, 105, 106, 108
Spurfowl, Red, 36, 77
Squirrel, 123: Palm, 88; Indian
  Giant, 45, 48, 50, 69, 71, 72,
  74; Striped Palm, 127
Starling, Rosy, 83, 94, 96, 103
Stilt, 123: Black-winged, 109

Stints, 101, 109: Little, 108; Temminck's, 108
Stonechat, 33, 56, 92, 106, 107, 111, 113, 126: Common, 124
Stork, 105: White, 104
Sunbird, 53, 95, 97, 113, 116, 119: Purple-rumped, 128
Swallow, 96, 114: Ashy Wood, 95; Red-rumped, 113
Swamphen, Purple, 118
Swift, 54, 57, 114: Alpine, 10, 36, 43, 60, 65, 71, 74; White-rumped, 36
Tailorbird, 119, 121, 128: Common, 77
Teal: Common, 33, 41, 52, 56, 84; Cotton, 56
Tern, 38, 70, 86, 90, 92, 93, 97, 100, 104, 113, 114, 123: Caspian, 38, 94, 98, 106, 111; Great-crested, 111, 112; Gull-billed, 95; Little, 92, 97; River, 98; Sandwich, 112; Whiskered, 95
Thick-knee, Eurasian, 95
Thrush, 45, 47, 63, 65: Blue Rock, 23, 59; Blue-capped Rock, 97; Malabar Whistling, 22, 25, 46, 47, 55, 60; Orange-headed Ground, 77; White-throated Ground, 46; White-throated, 30
Tiger, 27, 28, 40, 72, 127
Toads, 86
Tree-ant, Crematogaster, 127
Treepies, 29, 70
Treesnake, Bronzeback, 55
Tree-swift, Crested, 46
Trogon, Malabar, 24, 25, 50
Tropicbird, Red-billed, 114
Turnstone, Ruddy, 99, 111
Vinesnake, Green, 55
Viper: Bamboo Pit, 73; Malabar, 73; Russell's, 19, 59, 81; Saw-scaled, 19, 88, 113
Vulture, 74: Long-billed, 55, 59, 71; White-rumped, 55, 59, 98, 99
Wagtail, 94, 100, 111, 124, 126: Forest, 25; Grey, 83; Yellow, 83
Warbler, 15, 26, 33, 35, 41, 59, 77, 78, 87, 95, 96, 107, 116, 120, 124, 126: Clamorous Reed, 26, 90, 103, 104; Leaf, 47
Waterfowl, 16, 20, 85, 87
Waterhen, 52, 124: White-breasted, 79, 83
Weaver: Baya, 81, 111; Black-breasted, 105, 107, 108

Wheatear, Desert, 111, 112
Whimbrel, 38
Wigeon, 98
Wolf, 40
Woodpecker, 15, 21, 46, 64, 70, 73, 112: Heart-spotted, 25; Rufous, 22
Wryneck, Eurasian, 126
Yam fly, 25

PEOPLE & PLACES

Aarey Milk Colony, 76-79
Abdulali, Humayun, 112
Agardanda, 8, 114
Airoli Bridge, 102, 104
Airport Authority of India grounds, 124
Aksa, 92
Akshi, 112
Alibaug, 13, 110
All India Radio (AIR) estate, 80-81
Amba River, 58, 59
Ambedkar Garden, 118
Amby Valley, 59, 61
Arnala, 99
Arthur's Seat, 64
Badlapur Hills, 57, 84
Bandargaon, 38, 39
Bapane Reservoir, 87
Barvi Lake, 57
Bassein, 86, 87: Creek, 12, 18, 26, 27, 30, 86, 97; Fort, 86-88, 97
Bhairavgadh, 71
Bhandre Lake, 31
Bhandup BMC lagoons, 103, 104
Bhandvachamal, 49
Bhavan's College campus, 124
Bhayandar, 97
Bhima River, 73, 74
Bhimashankar, 9, 12, 53, 54, 55, 68, 72-74: temple, 74
Bhivpuri, 53
Bhoj Lake, 57
Bhoot Bangla, 23
BMC Versova Lagoon, 91
Bombay Environment Action Group, 42
Bombay Natural History Society (BNHS), 21, 47
Bombay Point, 63, 64
Boremal trail, 46
Bushi Lake, 60, 61
Byculla zoo. See Veermata Jijabhai Bhonsle Udyan
CEC (Conservation Education Centre), 21
Chackachamal, 49

Charkop, 82
Charlotte Lake, 43, 45
Chawni, 58
Chikhalgan trail, 49-50
Chinchoti, 26, 27, 29
Chota Kashmir Boat Club, 78
Colaba Woods, 128
Connaught Peak, 66
Cuffe Parade, 12, 128
Dahisar quarry, 25
Dan Beer Shiba trail, 64
Deonar, 103
Devkop Lake, 33, 100
Dhak, 53, 54, 74
Dharamtar Creek, 58, 109, 111
Dharivali Tekdi, 91, 92, 93
Dharnachigan trail, 50
Dhobi Waterfall, 64
Dhokavde pond, 112, 113
Duchess Road, 66
Durshet Lake, 59
Elephanta, 12, 13, 37-39, 109
Elphinstone Point, 64, 65
Esselworld, 116
Falkland Ride, 64
Forest Garden, 119
Funde, 109
Gadeshwar Lake, 84, 85
Gadgadyachamal, 49
Gadhi River, 84
Gargai river, 34, 36, 40
Gavalideo, 55
Gharapuri, 37
Ghatghar, 71
Ghatkopar, 121
Ghoni Lake, 56
Godrej Estates. See Pirojshanagar
Godrej Mangrove Project, 102
Godrej, SP, 122
Gomukh, 23
Gorai East trail, 97
Gunyachamal, 48, 49, 50
Gupt-Bhimashankar trail, 74
Hanging Gardens, 127
Harishchandragadh, 68, 69
Hiranandani Gardens, 119
IIT campus, 118-119
INS Shivaji, 61
Irshal, 45, 52
Jambulmal, 24
Jambulpada, 59
Jameson Ride, 64
Janjira, 48, 114
Jasai, 107, 108
Jawahar, 9, 34-36
Jawaharlal Nehru Port Trust (JNPT), 105
Jogger's Park, Navi Mumbai, 104
Juhu aerodrome, 124,

Juichandar, 87
Kakuli Lake, 56-57
Kamla Nehru Park, 127
Kandarpada trail, 95
Kanheri trail, 22-23
Kanheri, 19, 22, 25
Kankeshwar temple, 111
Karave pond, 106, 107
Karjat, 52-57, 72
Karnala Fort trail, 47
Karnala, 45, 46-47
Kashid, 113, 114
Kate's Point, 63, 66
Kelve, 13, 98, 100
Khandala, 60
Khandas, 53, 54, 55, 72, 73
Khokri, 114
Khopoli, 58
Kihim, 112
Killeshwar temple, 92
Kohoj, 32-33
Kolamb, 59
Konkan, 9, 10, 28; ports, 68, 70
Korlai, 26, 27, 48, 112, 113
Krishna River, 65, 66
Kulkarni, Vivek, 102, 103
Lady Willingdon Ride, 65
Lakeside Trail, 119
Limbdi Ride, 66
Lingmala Falls, 63
Lion's Point, 61
Lodwick Point, 64-65, 67
Lohagadh, 61
Lokhandwala Back Road, 90, 91
Lonavala Lake, 60, 61
Lonavala, 60
Madh Road, 90, 92
Mahabaleshwar, 9, 12, 60, 62-67
Mahadeo Temple, 29
Mahalaxmi Racecourse, 126
Maharashtra Nature Park, 122-123
Mahim Creek, 12, 122, 123
Mahim, 100
Mahuli Hills, 40, 41
Makunsar Creek, 100
Malabar Hill, 13, 127
Malad Creek, 11, 80, 90, 91, 93
Malshej Ghat, 12, 68-70
Malvani, 80
Mandwa, 110, 111
Mankhurd, 103
Manori Creek, 11, 82, 94, 116
Manpada, 26
Matheran, 12, 29, 42-45, 47, 52, 55, 57, 60, 84, 85; toy train, 42, 43
Metropolitan Region Development Authority, 122
MIDC Pipeline Road, 56, 57

Mithi River, 122
Modern Bakery trail, 79
Mortaka trail, 47
Mumbai region, 8: bird species, 8; fish species, 8, 11; flora, 12-14; mammal species, 8; monsoon, 15-16; pollution, 11, 16; reptile species, 8; rivers, 10; summer, 15; tree species, 13; winter, 14-15
Murud, 8, 13, 112, 114
Nagla block, 18, 26-27
Nagphani Point, 72, 74
Naigon, 87
Nanacha Angtha, 70, 71
Naneghat, 68, 70-71
Navi Mumbai, 54, 104
Navy Nagar, 12
New Zealand Hostel trail, 78
Nhava, 107
Nilje pond, 56
Nirmal, 98, 99
Nirvana Park, 119
Padar Killa, 54, 55, 74
Palasdhari Lake, 52
Panchgani Point, 66
Panchgani, 67
Panje, 109
Panorama Point, 43
Panvel Creek, 107
Panvel, 45, 46, 84-85: pond, 84, 85
Parsik Hills, 55
Patalganga River, 46, 47, 61
Peb, 85: Hills, 43
Pej River, 53, 54, 61
Pelhar Lake, 30, 31
Phansad Dam, 50
Phansad Wildlife Sanctuary, 48-50, 114
Pherozshah Mehta Garden. See Hanging Gardens
Pimpalgaon Reservoir, 70, 71
Pirojshanagar, 102, 120
Pisa, 63
Portuguese, 32, 86, 87, 92: churches, 110
Powai hills, 121
Powai Lake, 24, 76, 118, 119
Poynad, 111
Prabalgadh, 42, 45, 47, 85
Pratapgadh, 65, 67
Raj Bhavan, 127
Rajmachi, 53, 61
Rajwadi beach, 99
Revdanda, 113
Rewas, 110
Robber's Cave, 66
Ryewoods, 60

Sadanand Ashram, 31
Sahyadri Hills, 8, 10, 15, 40, 43, 45, 51-74
Saint Gonsalo Garcia School, 87
Sajan Nature Club, 34
Sajanpada, 33, 100
Sakhar Khadi, 112
Salim Ali Point, 20, 21
Salim Ali, 112, 123
Sanjay Gandhi National Park, 13, 18-27, 28, 76, 118, 121
Santosh Bhavan, 98
Sarasgadh, 59
Savratgan trail, 50
Sewri, 12, 13, 14, 101, 104
Shivaji, 40, 59, 67
Silonda trail, 25
South Gate trails, 19-21
Sudhagadh, 59
Supegaon, 49
Suriamal, 35, 36, 40
Takmak mountain, 31
Talzan, 82-83, 116
Tandulwadi, 98, 99, 100
Tansa Wildlife Sanctuary, 35, 36, 40-41
Tapola Road, 64, 66
Tata Electric Company, 128
Tata Power Company, 61
Thakurpada, 23
Thane Creek, 11, 14, 101, 102-104, 120, 121
Thane, 18, 26, 40
Tiger Spring, 65
Towers of Silence, 127
Trombay, 13
Tulsi Lake, 18, 19, 22, 24
Tulsi Valley, 24: trail, 23
Tungareshwar, 26, 27, 28-31: lower trail, 29; upper trail, 28, 29-31
Ulhas river, 53, 61
Uran, 105-109, 123
Uttan-Vashi islet, 92, 97
Vaishakhare, 70
Vaitarna River, 32, 40, 99, 100
Vasai, 87. See Bassein
Vashi Bridge, 102, 103
Vashi, 54
Vashind, 40, 41
Veermata Jijabhai Bhonsle Udyan, 125
Venna Lake, 63
Versova, 91
Vighaleshwar Lake, 98, 99
Vihar Lake, 18, 19, 21, 24
Vikhroli, 120
Wada, 35, 36
Water Kingdom, 116

Wavarli pond, 52
Western Ghats, 8, 18, 19, 50, 66, 73
Willingdon Sports Club, 126
Wilson Point, 66
World Wildlife Fund, 122
Yeur Hills, 26

PLANTS

Ain, 35
American Sumach, 125
Anjan, 43, 48, 49, 63
Arrowroot, 63: Indian, 66
Ashoka tree, 24, 78
Australian Acacia, 26, 109, 111
Australian Chestnut, 125
Babul, 110
Balsams, 16, 61, 63, 69:
    Common, 41, 82, 107
Bamboo, 12, 54, 107, 128
Banyan, 110, 113, 114, **123**
Baobab, 86, 88, 107, 114, 125
Barringtonia trees, 128
Bauhinia, Variegated, 26, 119
Bead-grass flowers, **63**
Begonia, Common, 25, 63
Belleric Myrobalan, 127
Ber. *See* Indian Jujube
Betel-nut, 112
Black Plum, 24, 43, 60, 63, 82, 110
Black Siris, 41, 47
Bladderwort, 63
Blue Fountain Bush, 47, 61
Bonfire Tree, 15, 36, 78, 79, 95, 128
Bottle-brush tree, 78
Brazil Jute, 13, 82, **83**
Bulrush, 84
Butterfly Bean, 82
Cactus, 18, 22, 78
Calabash Tree, 125
Cannonball, 121
Cashewnut, 92, 96
Castor Oil Plant, 13, 90, 118
Casuarina, 13, **98**, 100, 110, 112, 114
Charcoal Tree, 127
Chiku, 92, 96, 97
Christ's Thorn, 35, 90
Cockscomb, Silver Spiked, **85**, 107
Coconut, 13, 92, 112
Common Borage, 107
Common Chaste Tree, 114
Common Marsh Buckwheat, **21**
Congress Grass, 13
Copper Pod, 19, 26, 79, 125
Cup-n-Saucer plant, **49**
Date Palm, 86, 87

Devil's Claw, 16, 82
Devil's Tree, **117**
Entada, 48
Eucalyptus, 37, 67
Fern Tree, 125
Ficus, 86, 114, 116
Flamboyant, 26, 37, 79, 125
Flame Amherstia, 125
Flame of the Forest, 15, 37, 41, 47, **52**, 53, 54, 119, 128
Flowering Murdals, **114**
Forest Barleria, **31**
Fungus, bioluminescent, **73**
Gans, 48
Ghost Tree, 127
Glory Lily, **35**, 78, 82, 107
Graham's Groundsel, 16, 61, 63, 66, 69
Gulmohar. *See* Flamboyant
Haldu, 27, 37, 41, 47
Hedge Bower, 95
Hedge Caper, 23
Hill Jambul, 43
Hill Turmeric, 63
Indian Coral, 15, 119
Indian Cork Tree, 128
Indian Jujube, 81, 83, 110
Indian Laburnum, 15, **16**, **121**, 128
Indian Medlar, 43, 60
Indian Rosewood. *See* Sissoo
Indian Saltwort, 102
Ipomoea, 84
Ironwood Tree, 128
Jacaranda, 37
Jackfruit, 97
Jamun. *See* Black Plum
Jarul. *See* Queen's Flower
Kadamb, 121
Kalamb, 99
Kapok. *See* White Silk Cotton
Karanj, 41, 47, 82, 119
Karaya, 37, 41, 78, 119
Karvi, 24, 47, **61**, 72
Khejri, 110
Kino, 37: Indian, 128
Kleinhovia hospita, 125
Kokam, 43, 60
Krishna's Buttercup, 125
Kusum tree, 15, 41, 47
Lantana, Common, 13
Lily: Forest Spider, 15; Glory, **35**; 78, 82, 107; Pink-striped Trumpet, 15, 21
Long-tailed Habernaria, 47
Lotus, 56, 84
Mahua, 35, 41
Mal grassland, 48, 49
Mango, 37, 82, 87, 92, 93, 96, 97
Mangrove Beanstalk, 95, 102

Mangrove, 10, 11-12, 38, 109, 111, 112: White, 11, 90; *at* creeksides, 26, 27, 82, 90, 92, 93, 94, 95, 96, 97, 102, 103, 104, 116; *at* Pirojshanagar, 120; *at* Sewri, 101
Manila Tamarind, 110
Marigold, 99
Marsh Barbel, 55, 118
Marsh Glory, 55, 84, 90, 118
Mauritius Grass, 76
Myrobalan, 41
Orchid, Foxtail, **61**; ground, **24**
Oriental Sesame, 16, 82
Palm: Date, 86, 87; Fish Tail, 78; Palmyras, 13, 94; Talipot, 125; Toddy, 92, 95; Traveller's, 78
Paper Flower Climber, 40
Par Jamun, 63
Para. *See* Mauritius grass
Parkinsonia aculeate, 109
Passion Flower, 82
Pipal, 92
Portia tree, 113
Potato Tree, 121
Potatoes, 62
Prosopis. *See* Khejri
Purging Nut, 114
Queen's Flower tree, **77**, 78
Red Silk Cotton, 14, 21, 37, 46, 79, 127
Rudraksh, 125
Sea Holly, 37, **92**, 93, 102
Sensitive Smithia, 16, 26, 61
Shore Purselane, 37, 95, 102
Silver Oak, 67
Silver-spiked Cockscomb, 16
Sissoo, 26, 128
Soccerball Tree, 119
Socks Tree, 121
Spiral Ginger, 78, **79**
Spotted Gliricidia, 19
Stinkwood Tree, 125
Strawberries, 62, 66
Su-babul, 26, 109
Sunflowers, 99
Talipot Palm, 125
Tamarind, 37, 86, 87, 92
Teak, 37, 41, 47, 127
Toddy Palm, 92
Toothbrush Plant, 91, 93, 96, 103
Touch Me Not, 82-83
Tree species, 13
Water Hyacinth, 118
Water Lily, 56, 84
Whistling Pine. *See* Casuarina
White Day Glory, 91
White Silk Cotton, 128
Yellow Silk Cotton, 128

ISBN 81-7508-359-X

TEXT & PHOTOGRAPHS

© 2003 Sunjoy Monga
unless otherwise indicated

PUBLISHED BY

India Book House Pvt Ltd
Mahalaxmi Chambers
22 Bhulabhai Desai Road
Mumbai 400 026, India
Tel 91 22 2495 3827   Fax 91 22 2493 8406
E-mail publishing@ibhworld.com